LIFE.NOW.

Books by
Shannon Kubiak Primicerio
FROM BETHANY HOUSE PUBLISHERS

Being a Girl Who Leads
Being a Girl Who Loves
Being a Girl Who Serves
God Called a Girl
The Divine Dance

LIFE.NOW.

overcoming the ten obstacles
that derail your dreams

SHANNON & MICHAEL
PRIMICERIO

BETHANYHOUSE
Minneapolis, Minnesota

Published by Bethany House Publishers
11400 Hampshire Avenue South
Bloomington, Minnesota 55438

Bethany House Publishers is a division of
Baker Publishing Group, Grand Rapids, Michigan.

Printed in the United States of America

ISBN-13: 978-0-7642-0314-5
ISBN-10: 0-7642-0314-2

Library of Congress Cataloging-in-Publication Data

Primicerio, Shannon Kubiak.
    Life now: overcoming the ten obstacles that derail your dreams / Shannon & Michael Primicerio.
       p. cm.
    Summary: "Focusing on ten factors that often prevent young people from living the lives they dream of, this guide offers practical tips to overcome the obstacles and find the resources to accomplish their dreams while also discovering how those goals fit into God's overall plan for their lives"—Provided by publisher.
    ISBN-13: 978-0-7642-0314-5 (hardcover : alk. paper)
    ISBN-10: 0-7642-0314-2 (hardcover: alk. paper)
    1. Dreams—Religious aspects—Christianity. 2. Christian life. I. Primicerio, Michael. II. Title.
    BR115.D74P75   2007
    248.4—dc22   2006038326

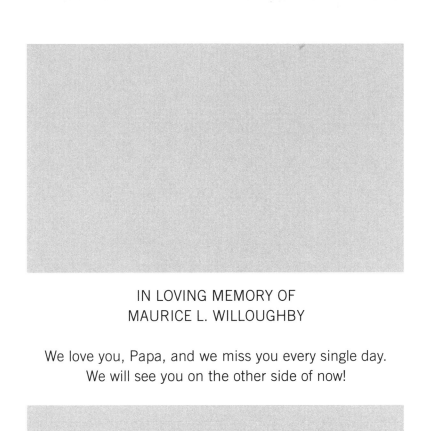

IN LOVING MEMORY OF
MAURICE L. WILLOUGHBY

We love you, Papa, and we miss you every single day.
We will see you on the other side of now!

CONTENTS

YOUR MOMENT IS NOW 9

1. WHAT IF IT DOESN'T WORK OUT? 15

2. WHAT IF NO ONE CLAPS FOR ME? 29

3. WHO AM I AWAY FROM HOME? 43

4. AM I WEIRD FOR WANTING MORE? 59

5. AM I REALLY IN CHARGE OF MY OWN LIFE? 75

6. HOW DO I GET THERE? 91

7. HOW DO I FUND MY DREAMS? 105

8. DO I REALLY THINK I CAN? 123

9. WHEN I THINK OF MY FUTURE, WHAT DO I SEE? 139

10. HOW DO I KNOW GOD'S WILL? 153

APPENDIX 167

ABOUT THE AUTHORS 169

YOUR MOMENT IS NOW

Have you ever felt stuck? We know from experience that is one of the worst feelings in the world. Yet for those of us in our twenties, it is a feeling that has become all too familiar. At a time when we should be forging ahead and accomplishing all we've ever dreamed of, many of us find ourselves simply trying to get unstuck. Or worse yet, sitting back in frustration, assuming that being stuck is our lot in life. *Is it ever going to get better than this?* Our minds race, yet our feet stand still, firmly planted where it is safe, and we are stuck.

The thought of getting from where we are to where we want to go in life is almost too much to bear. We begin to think it is virtually impossible. And it is—if you choose to look at the big picture apart from the smaller, more reasonable steps it will take to get there. Getting unstuck will happen only one way: by choosing to deliberately live your life—dreams and goals included—*now*.

Easy for you to say, you might think. But what you probably don't realize is that this book was written by two people in their twenties who discovered a way to get unstuck and want desperately to share it. We're not experts from another generation. We haven't yet "arrived." You want proof? We live in an apartment and drive cars more than five years old. Enough said.

Although we may not have found the latest get-rich-quick scheme, we have found the secret to getting unstuck. It's the secret that allowed me (Shannon) to sign a contract for my first book when I was only twenty and release my tenth book by the age of twenty-five.

It's the secret that allowed Michael to begin a career he merely likes (selling insurance), which provides him with a generous income and a flexible schedule so he can pursue a life he truly loves (writing and teaching God's truths to others). Needless to say, we think it works. We're sure you have heard of the analogy of bridge building before, and usually it sounds slow and rather boring: "Take baby steps to get where you want to go." Yuck. Our view of bridge building isn't like that. Early in our twenties we began putting our heart and soul into everything we did. We gave our all to anything that would help catapult us ahead on the bridge toward our dreams. Passion was poured into everything we did. In our minds we weren't just building bridges, we were watching as our dreams came alive with each step we daringly took toward where we wanted to go.

As a result, we learned to make intentional decisions that helped us live with purpose and get closer to achieving our goals each and every day. We call this concept *living the bridge*. One step at a time we started toward our goals. And while we were building, we kept right on living, until one day we eventually found ourselves living our dreams.

Sounds easy, doesn't it? Well, it's not. But it *is* possible.

And at least possible is an easy enough place to start. We have found that there are primarily ten things that affect our ability to live the lives we dream of. Throughout the book you will see these ten things referred to as Challenge Points. Each chapter will focus on how to meet each Challenge and get closer to living your dreams. Let's briefly touch on them now, and then we will spend the rest of the book taking a deeper look at them.

Fear: It takes on many shapes and forms and can sometimes creep into our lives in subtle ways. Maybe you are afraid of making sacrifices in order to pursue your dreams, or maybe you are deathly afraid you will fail if you get out there and try. If we don't learn to handle fear correctly, we will never get beyond the first step.

The Approval of Others: We all crave it. Those of us who claim we don't are liars. Because of this, we tend to stick with people we are comfortable with or those we have known for a long time. If they aren't willing to support us in our dream, we abandon it. As a result we become "secure" by being part of a group even if that group is seemingly going nowhere.

The Comforts of Home: By nature most people are not risk takers. We like to be comfortable. And home—wherever that may be—is usually one of the most comforting places we know. Perhaps you still have the benefit of living under your parents' roof rent free, or you attend the same church with the same friends you have spent your whole life knowing. Things like these aren't easy to leave. But if you have a dream that requires venturing out, these are things you will have to part with to some degree. Just think of it this way: There is a new home somewhere out there just waiting to offer you its comforts.

A Normal and Average Life: Normal is a relative word, we'll give you that. But *average* is something that can be defined pretty easily. It means we are just like everyone else. We do what's expected—what's been done before, what others are doing. And chances are, in doing this we are selling ourselves short. In all honesty, no one wants to be remembered for being average; we want to be remembered for being excellent. But you have to abandon average to get to excellent.

> No one wants to be remembered for being average; we want to be remembered for being excellent.

A Sense of Control: Come on now, who *doesn't* like to be in control? Although many times the sense of control we do have is really false, we still like to believe that we are in charge of what happens to us and that we are in control of what is going on in our lives. Even if our dreams are absent and our lives are less than we desire them to be, we want to claim that we allowed it to happen and that we didn't really want to pursue our dreams anyway.

Knowledge of Where to Start: Having the knowledge of where to start when it comes to getting from where you are to where you want to go can be tough—especially if your dream is big. That's why breaking your dream down into smaller, easier-to-reach goals is important. Just like stepping-stones, these small goals will ultimately lead you all the way to living out your dream.

The Money to Make It Happen: Life takes money, and

many times a lot of it. Chances are, if you are in your twenties, you just don't have it. Thanks to student loans, credit cards, and automobiles—and our dependency on them—twentysomethings have now been dubbed "Generation Debt." But even with bank accounts hovering just above zero and interest rates soaring through the roof, we can get a handle on our finances and make progress toward being able to fund the things we desperately want to see happen in our lives.

The Motivation to Do It: There is something risky about pursuing our dreams. We might fall on our faces or go broke (if it is possible to get more broke than we already are), or we might succeed—and sometimes *that* is the scariest thing of all since it would change absolutely everything. Many times it can be difficult to actually get motivated to step up and give the lives we desperately want to live a try, and it can be even harder to stay motivated if our dreams don't come together all at once.

The Vision to Follow Through: Making it all the way from where we are to where we want to go is not going to happen overnight. Sometimes it takes more work than we realized when we started; other times we have to go through long periods of failure and discouragement before achieving success. Quitting is easy. It's continuing on that is tough. That's why having a vision of what life will look like on the other side of your dream is absolutely vital.

A Knowledge of How Your Dream Fits Into God's Will for You: Many times we try to write our dreams off as a crazy notion or a child's silly musings. But chances are the dream you hold dearest—the one you just cannot seem to shake—is more than that. It very well could be God's will for your life. If you don't take a chance, an absolute risk, and get out there and live it out, the world will be at a loss. More often than not our dreams are part of God's plan, and it's just a matter of letting Him put the pieces together and show us how they fit.

These ten things are important to talk about and wrestle with, because it is only in wrestling with them that we will be able to break free from the chains that hold us back from living the lives we desperately long to live. It is our hope that this book gives you insight and encouragement as you reflect on the topics discussed and you emerge from the shadows to embrace the life you were destined for. Each chapter includes reflection questions and an action point to help you start making progress toward living your life *now*. The appendix in the back of the book lists a few additional resources you may find helpful, and if you visit our Web site, *www.yourmomentisnow.com,* you will be able to find a more extensive list of resources that may help you on your quest.

Now is the time to get unstuck, build your bridge, and get from where you are to where you want to go. If we can do it, you can too. And we'll tell you how. The clock is ticking. We're all running out of time. Your moment is *now.*

Challenge Point #1:
Fear

WHAT IF IT DOESN'T WORK OUT?

> **❝** *Take care which rut you choose. You will be in it for* **❞**
> *the next 25 miles.*
> —*A sign at a fork in the road in Canada*

Imagine living your whole life dreaming about one thing yet never really doing it. As awful as that sounds, many of us do just that. We live our lives in the prison of unrealized dreams. We look out on a world that promises much yet delivers little. And we feel shortchanged and cheated. We are left wanting more and settling for less.

Many times we blame it on age. We convince ourselves that our dreams aren't meant for our twenties—they are meant for that day when we finally "grow up." Chances are most of us will never really grow up. That doesn't mean we won't grow *old*; it just means we will find ourselves at our eightieth birthday party still talking about the very same things we dream of doing today, and they will still be just that—dreams. The "I want to be such-and-such when I grow up" mentality may work when you are five, but let's be honest here. It's just plain stale by the time you reach twenty-five.

Fear: The Number One Roadblock

All of us are afraid of something. And in an indirect way, many of us are afraid of our own dreams. They seem too big or too far out of reach. They might stretch us and change us, and what if we don't like who we become on the other side? We demonstrate this fear in one of two ways: We talk openly about our dreams and how we are going to make it big one day—yet we never do anything to get there. Or we go into hiding, sharing our dreams with no one because we don't ever want to be encouraged to come out of our shells.

We have met many people who fall into the first category. Both in our personal lives and in our ministry, we have encountered countless people who tell us all about what they are going to do one day—yet they aren't currently taking a single step to get there. What they want to do differs, but how they approach it is the same. For instance, there is the wannabe lawyer who keeps taking breaks from going to school, or the girl who wants to be a writer but has decided she's too busy to take writing classes or attend a writers' conference. The list could go on for pages.

> *There is a huge difference between what a person* can *do and what he or she* will *do.*

Every time these people, and others like them, open their mouths and tell us about these dreams they are going to accomplish, we want to look at them and say, "Are you *really*?" It's not that we don't believe they can—it's that we aren't convinced they will. There is a huge difference between what a person *can* do and what he or she *will* do. When it comes to pursuing your dream, it is going to take a whole lot of willpower and hard work to get there. Just because you *can* get to where you want to go doesn't mean you *will*.

A lot of Christians adapt the mentality, "If it's God's will, then it will happen." While that is true, that doesn't eliminate the fact that we must obey to get the blessing. We'll bet that you have never met a lawyer without a law degree or a doctor without a medical degree. God's sovereign will over our lives is not an excuse for us to be lazy. We can miss out on some of His blessings by our own inactivity. If God is moving, you've got to be moving with Him or you may never get from where you are to where you want to go.

The more Michael and I (Shannon) listen to seemingly aimless people talk, the more we realize the thing that holds them back is simply fear. They are so afraid of what might happen if they actually try to do what they desperately want to do that they just cannot bring themselves to do it. The other type of fearful person remains silent, quietly watching others live out their dreams while secretly wishing he or she could do that too. People like that might buy a book like this and hide it because they wouldn't want anyone else knowing that they do have dreams or that they are thinking of pursuing them.

No matter what category you fall into, fear (in regard to our dreams) usually takes on one of three forms: the fear of failing, the fear of what others will think, or the fear of change. Let's take a closer look at all three.

What If I'm Not Good Enough?

All of us are afraid of failing in some way or another. The concept of finally attempting to reach for our dreams and falling flat on our face as a result is not appealing to anyone. Oddly enough, we think it is safer to leave our dreams tucked away in the secret places of our minds and hearts where no one can touch them and we can't possibly ever fail. We think it is better to not try and not fail than it is to fail when we do try.

Growing up, I (Shannon) was painfully shy in public places, although my family would tell you I was pretty outgoing behind closed doors. In fast food restaurants I was too shy to go up to the counter and ask for ketchup packets. Trying to break me of my shyness and insecurity, my parents stopped doing this for me, hoping that I would emerge from my shell. Instead I ate my French fries without ketchup.

If you had told me as a ten-year-old that I would one day have a career involving public speaking and making myself vulnerable by writing books, I would have told you there was just no way. As a painfully private person, I wouldn't have been able to imagine sharing so much of my life with other people—perfect strangers, no less. I am so private, in fact, that I was a third of the way through writing my first book before my own parents even knew I was *thinking about* writing a book. I'm not a person who likes spotlights or center stage. I seriously considered canceling my own bridal shower because I didn't want to be the center of attention for so many people.

Those who know me best know that I still get nervous when I send a book proposal to a publisher hoping to get another contract; that public speaking still kind of freaks me out; and that strangers reading my thoughts in my books sometimes makes me uneasy. Pursuing your dreams doesn't mean you are no longer afraid. It just means you don't give in to that fear.

Recently I was interviewed on a radio program where I was asked about fear. "How do people get over fear?" The radio host's question sounded automatic, as if he had asked it of a countless number of guests. Judging by the hesitation before his response, I could tell my answer caught him by surprise.

> *Pursuing your dreams doesn't mean you are no longer afraid.*

"I don't think you ever really get over fear," I said to him after taking a deep breath. "You learn not to give in to it. That knot you have in your stomach may very well always be there. You just need to learn to realize that God is bigger than that knot, and if He has called you to do something, He is going to take your hand and lead you all the way through it. Every time you think you can't do something, realize that you are right. You can't, but God can. Because of that you don't need to give in to fear."

If you can't but God can, then you have no reason to be afraid of failing. You are guaranteed to fail—but God isn't. And if God has given you a dream and He has opened the doors for you to pursue it, then you have to take a risk and bank on the fact that God just cannot fail. I know you think it is easier said than done, and it is. You have to take risks if you ever want to get from where you are to where you want to go—especially since dreams tend to come together in pieces rather than all at once, like we imagine they will.

When I attended my first writers' conference, I was a

19

twenty-year-old college student who had read one, maybe two, books on how to write a book. And with a proposal in my shaky hands, I sat down and met with an editor who made me a published author in less than a year. If you think I wasn't scared to go to that conference and meet with that editor, you are absolutely crazy.

The odds were in favor of my *not* getting a contract at that conference. In fact, the odds were even in favor of my becoming the laughingstock of the conference. I was the youngest attendee by years, and I sat in a crowd with people who had been receiving rejection letters for my entire lifetime. I could almost hear the whispers in the room: "Look at the college kid who thinks she can write a book. . . ." And I actually did hear a few less than encouraging comments.

Prior to the conference, I almost talked myself out of going a hundred times—and I only talked myself into going once, on the day of the actual event. Every other day I thought about going I was ready to chicken out. But I went, and my entire life changed as a result. At twenty years old I was handed a ticket to pursue my dreams. Had I stayed home instead, I would have missed a huge part of God's plan for me, and I would more than likely be unsatisfied and frustrated with whatever job I would be working now. I had a dream that was so real to me that it demanded I do something about it. Chances are you have a dream that is demanding something of you as well. Only you are still trying to drown it out as you give in to fear.

I'm living my dream for one reason alone: I took a risk and trusted God. It's time you started taking risks and trusting God too.

What Will They Think?

The fear of failing is usually directly linked to the fear of what other people will think. After all, failure is usually measured by someone else's standard (or what we *assume* is someone else's standard) and not our own. But we have to ask ourselves, "Who are these people we are listening to? Do they even have dreams for their own lives, or are they just as bound by fear as I am?" Many times the loudest critics are those who are the most afraid. Because of their own fear of stepping out and pursuing their passions, they automatically attack anyone who takes a risk and attempts to accomplish his or her dreams. Critics are fearful people who spend their lives trying to make others fearful too. If they can make you too afraid to pursue your dreams, they feel less guilty about not pursuing theirs.

We recently read the story of a young woman who decided she no longer wanted to be a hairdresser. Instead she wanted to pursue her dream of being an engineer. "I lost a lot of friends during the whole thing," she said. "People become jealous when you decide to do what no one thought you would or could. You just have to push through."[1]

Success isn't always contagious, but the desire for success is. Being around someone who is living out his or her dreams and passions has one of two effects on other people. It motivates them to pursue their dreams too, or it causes them to claim life is not fair since they don't have the boldness to venture out and pursue their own dreams.

You cannot give other people permission to control

---

[1]Keith Ferrazzi, *Never Eat Alone* (New York: Double Day, 2005), 38.

your dreams—which is exactly what you do when you let the fear of their opinions govern whether you actually set out and pursue them. If you let other people control your dreams, they will essentially control you, making you as miserable and unhappy as they are.

We also have to be careful, however, not to fall into the trap of *assuming* that people do or don't approve of our choices. It's been said, "I am not who I think I am. I am not who you think I am. I am who I think you think I am." Most of what we assume other people think about us just simply isn't true.

When Michael first began working with the company he is with now, he talked to me often about how insignificant he felt in a nationwide company that has employees in almost every state.

"I doubt anyone even knows my name," he used to lament over and over again. At the first company event I ever attended with him, he was greeted—by name—by his regional manager (who oversees production in several states) within our first two minutes in the door. No name tags. There wasn't even anyone else around who could have whispered Michael's name to him as we walked in. Not only did someone know Michael by name—*upper management* knew him by name. His assumption that he was insignificant proved to be untrue. Many times our assumptions prove to be the same.

Comfortable Where You Are

One of the main reasons other people can be so discouraging when it comes to our dreams is simply because most people are afraid of change. Just before we got married, I (Michael) desired to make a career change. I had worked on staff in youth ministry at our church for the last three years, and honestly, I stayed because it was comfortable. I loved the environment. I liked the people. And after that many years, youth ministry was as easy for me as breathing. Having interned at my church for so long, the pastor was ready to offer me a full-time position when I got engaged, and I gladly accepted it. It was an ideal solution for a guy like me looking to take a bride and provide for her. Sure, our income would have been sparse, but we would have made it work. One short month into this position, I knew it *wasn't* made for me. I had to get out. My very life depended on it. And with my wedding quickly approaching, I began to look for (and pray about) any and every possible way to get out of this position and into something—anything—else. Shannon and I considered everything from moving out of state so I could go to seminary to working with a friend at a local warehouse while still volunteering at church.

Door after door closed for me—except one: leaving ministry altogether and accepting a position in the secular business world. Having spent the previous three years of my life wanting to be a pastor, venturing out into a commission-based sales job was a stretch for me. At first I was uncomfortable. Not only would this job involve leaving ministry, but it also meant packing my bags and leaving the small town I had grown up in for the fast-paced city life in Orange County.

The more Shannon and I prayed about it, the more the Lord seemed to open the doors. The flexibility and income my new job would provide would allow Shannon and me to really expand her (and eventually our) ministry of writing and speaking. If that wasn't enough evidence that God was in all of this, impossible things started to happen. I passed my state licensing exam on the first try (which is rare) and found that I actually had a knack for sales. Immediately I started winning companywide contests and gaining influence over my colleagues—many who are a lot older than I am. There were many opportunities to share my faith, and people were willing to listen simply because I was a successful salesman. Finally things were starting to come together for me, and I was excited.

But then the critics started to speak—and there seemed to be so many of them. "You are abandoning God's will for your life by leaving the ministry," they said to me. "You'll never be any good at sales," others chimed in. The worst of it, though, came through the comments spoken behind my back. People were very loud about how wrong they thought my choices were. But I had to go forward, knowing I was doing exactly what God wanted me to do *no matter what others thought.*

There are going to be critics in life. That's a guarantee. Many times these people can rile anger in us unlike anyone else. More often than not they are people who know us well, so they know where to hit us where it will hurt the worst. But we cannot let them take control of our future by making us afraid to go forward. In moments like this, it has to be us and God—and no one else. If we trust Him in moments like these, He will prove His faithfulness to us.

I do, however, want to make something clear. I am not in any way discouraging seeking godly counsel. Proverbs

11:14 talks about having safety in many counselors. In my job transition I sought counsel from many people—Shannon, my pastor, my parents, my in-laws. Seek counsel from those whose opinions you trust, and listen to those who will listen to the heart of God on your behalf. Once you have done that, know that you can confidently throw out the opinions of everyone else.

Avoiding a Rut

Many times, we as people tend to gravitate toward what is familiar. We seek to stick with what we know. Because of this, many of us end up in ruts. And once we are in a rut, it is hard to get out. Sticking with what is comfortable is how people wind up having a midlife crisis. They spend so long playing it safe that life passes them by. They wind up forty or fifty years old, still desperately wanting to do what they wanted to do at twenty. So they pursue it. And everyone around them looks at them like they are nuts since they never breathed a word about these secret dreams (now called a crisis) to anyone before.

There are several ways to determine whether you are currently in a rut. They are:

- You are in a job with no advancement opportunities.
- You have not moved significantly toward any educational goals.
- Your finances have not increased since this time last year. (You are really in a rut if they have decreased.)
- You have not met any new people in months and haven't made a new friend in over a year.
- You are out of college, still living with your parents, and do not have a solid move-out date nailed down.

If you are in a rut at this point in your life, get out. Get out and run as far away from that rut as you possibly can. Make any necessary changes in where you live, work, or go to church. Find new friends if necessary. Do whatever it takes to get out of your rut. Getting out isn't enough. If you stay too close to your rut, you might be tempted to jump back in it when the going gets tough or when others who are stuck in the rut call out to you and tell you how much fun you are missing.

Don't be afraid to seek help in getting out of a rut. A few years ago I (Michael) used to drive up in the hills near my house to get alone with God and spend some time reading my Bible and praying. I drove (and still drive) a four-door Honda Civic, which usually isn't a problem. But on this particular morning, after it had just rained, my car got stuck in a rut. There was no way out on my own. So with barely any reception, I called my brother from my cell phone and asked if he and a friend would come help pull me out. Using pieces of cardboard and whatever else we could find to stick under my tires, the three of us got my car out. I couldn't have done it on my own.

Sometimes going forward, and getting out of a rut, involves enlisting a trusted friend, family member, or pastor who can pull us out and help us make the changes necessary to get from where we are to where we want to go. You might be surprised at just how many people would be willing to help you if you will just ask. Currently Shannon and I know a guy who has made some poor choices and has a rough road ahead of him. We love him a lot and pray for him constantly. And he knows those things. But in the past he hasn't been interested in our help. This time we're hoping (and praying) he will finally bring himself to ask. If he does, we will be more than willing to go out of our way to help him out of his rut. Don't be afraid to ask for help if you need it. Change is not easy. If it were, people wouldn't be so afraid of it.

Getting from where you are in life to where you want to go is a lot like crossing a bridge. Many times when you start out on a bridge you cannot see the other side—although you know where you are going. That's why the process of getting to where you want to go in life is tricky. You are working toward a goal, a dream. You know the steps you are taking are leading you closer and closer to that goal or that dream. But you cannot see it yet. And "seeing is believing," as they say.

But the Bible tells us something different. Second Corinthians 5:7 says, "We live by believing and not by seeing." This belief is not in ourselves. If it were, we should all quit before we even start. Our belief needs to be in a dream-giving God who delights in stretching His children and taking them so far out of their comfort zones that they have to trust Him. Dreams are not simple things we could easily accomplish on our own. Things we can do on our own don't involve faith, they don't involve risk, and they don't involve fear. They don't stretch us, they don't break us, and they don't add any adventure to life.

So if you want to live a life without faith and growth, then feel free to put this book down and stop reading. This book isn't for people without dreams. It's for those who not only have dreams but are ready to realize them *now*.

FOR FURTHER THOUGHT:

1. Is there an area in your life where you are giving in to fear? If so, what is it and why are you fearful?
2. Have you been trying to win the approval of critics in your life? If so, how can you begin to break free from that?
3. Have you ever used your age as an excuse not to pursue your dreams and goals? If so, what age are you waiting for before beginning to pursue them? Why?
4. Are there any ruts in your life? If so, what steps can you begin taking to get out of them?
5. Do you have someone in your life who can help you out of your ruts? If not, where can you begin looking for someone like that?

DO IT NOW

Share at least one of your deepest goals and dreams with another person. Honestly express any fears you may have and ask that person to pray for you and hold you accountable to not letting fear win in your life. Schedule a consistent time to check back in with this person so you can make him or her aware of your progress.

> **"** *Don't think you're on the right road* **"**
> *just because it's a well-beaten path.*
> —*Unknown*

For me (Shannon), the fall of 2005 marked a time of radical change in my life. Michael and I had just gotten married and moved to a new city, and I had scheduled a large block of time to just be. There were no speaking engagements, no writing deadlines, no small groups to attend, and no ministry of any kind that needed to be done. It was a time to tend my soul. And although I didn't know it then, it was a time that would forever mark the beginning of my emancipation. Finally I would be able to take active steps to break free from the need for approval from other people.

I had just come off a year of consistent writing projects, planning a wedding, and a full plate of speaking engagements—all while holding down a part-time job in church ministry. In all of those areas there had been people to please: "Can you have one book done every three months?" "I know you said your wedding is an adults-only affair, but that doesn't mean my kids can't attend, does it?" "I know our event is planned for right after your honeymoon, but we still really want you to come speak to us."

"I know you teach both the junior high and high school girls' Bible studies, but we really need you to take on more counseling appointments."

Like every other over-committed person out there, I had found myself burned out and tired. I honestly considered quitting it all—giving up my dream of writing—and escaping to a cubicle somewhere just so I could relieve myself from these burdens and pressures. But as I set out for job interviews with résumé in hand, I realized my problem wasn't with where all of these demands were coming from. The problem was with how I responded to them. And thus my path to freedom began.

With a big thick marker in hand, I sat down and mapped out a wall chart of life goals in every category ranging from devotional activity to financial goals to relational goals and health and fitness goals. I even wrote down my goal to get a certain amount of sleep every night. Under the heading "Personal Growth" I wrote down four things: be me, take more risks, be free, and let go.

What I truly wanted was the freedom to be myself, not some mutated version of what others thought I should be. I wanted to write and speak only what I wanted to write and where I wanted to speak. And I wanted the freedom to let go of the pain that had come as a result of losing the approval of other people. Essentially, I wanted to be less frazzled and more alive.

Slowly and steadily things became clearer to me. Freedom, for me, started with one word. Two tiny letters, used properly, opened up a world to me where life finally made sense and I could breathe again. *No.* It felt good to say it and even better to mean it. I was on my way.

The first person I said no to was another author who had approached me several years ago about partnering on a lucrative project that would have been very beneficial for both of us, and in many ways it would have been a dream for me. But as the time approached to move forward with what she and I discussed, I knew God was telling me to say no. Tired and weary from always saying yes, I obeyed. Her response to my no was gracious: "Oh, Shannon, I can see you are truly seeking God on this one. Good for you." Months later when I said no yet again—this time to someone who wanted me to speak at an event she was planning—the answer was a lot less gracious.

"Well, I am surprised you would say that," she e-mailed me, as if what I had done was absolutely absurd. It was then I learned that saying no isn't always easy. But . . . even in moments when it is not easy, it is still necessary—vital even—to our survival and our spiritual growth.

> Saying no isn't always easy. But . . . even in moments when it is not easy, it is still necessary—vital even—to our survival and our spiritual growth.

Other people's opinions always seem to be a driving force in our lives. We crave affirmation in the same way we crave air—we need it to survive. People, by nature, are insecure. The number one fear of all Americans is public speaking. You know why? Because we are afraid of what other people will think of us if we get up onstage with something to say. *What if they don't agree? What if I stutter? What if I forget what I am supposed to say?* We are absolutely haunted by what others *might* think of us. Don't you think it is odd that people as a whole are so controlled by what *might* happen instead of being concerned about things that *will* happen—like what *will* happen to them when they die?

The fear of public speaking and the opinions of others can be traced all the way back to the Old Testament and the life of Moses. When God instructs Moses to go to Pharaoh to demand the release of the Israelites from captivity, and to tell the Israelites that God will set them free, Moses answers God by saying, "Look, they won't believe me! They won't do what I tell them. They'll just say, 'The Lord never appeared to you'" (Exodus 4:1).

The deepest desire of each of us is to be known and accepted for who we are. *Who we are* includes our dreams and goals. Living someone else's idea of what your life should be may make you feel accepted, but this acceptance is not for yourself—it's for someone else. Famed actress Judy Garland once said, "Always be a first-rate version of yourself, rather than a second-rate version of somebody else."

Each of us needs to get to a place in our lives where we are comfortable with who we are and who God has made us. We need to be comfortable *outside* of other people's approval. Because if we choose to pursue our dreams and get from where we are to where we want to go in life, there is a guarantee that other people's approval *isn't* something we will always have.

Stop Asking for Permission

Once I started saying no, I began wondering why I hadn't said it more often. Even when I had said it in the past, I said it with guilt. It wasn't long before I discovered that I had spent many of my early adult years waiting for permission to say no. Finally it occurred to me that, just as an elementary school student is trained to raise his or her hand to ask for permission before doing something as necessary as going to the rest room, I had lived my life with my hand raised in the air waiting for people to grant me permission to do something as vital as saying no. I've got news for you: We're not in elementary school anymore. In fact, we're not even kids anymore. We do not need to raise our hands and ask for permission before doing something like pursuing our dreams and what we honestly believe to be God's will for our lives.

I've met countless young people who have been waiting for permission. Some were waiting for permission to attend cosmetology school instead of a university. Others wanted to leave their small town and pursue a career in music. Some simply wanted to take a job that wasn't connected to the family business. In each of these cases there was a heart crying out for freedom, but the sense of needing to be granted permission before moving forward caused them to remain shackled.

Chances are most of us grew up not wanting to disappoint someone—whether it was our parents, a mentor, a teacher, or even a pastor. And as we got older the list of people we didn't want to disappoint continued to grow: a significant other, a boss, people at church, our friends. The list could go on and on. And with the longer list came more people we would need permission from before stepping out and living the lives we truly dream of. A lot of this boils down to the expectations we think others have set for us.

Great Expectations

Recently I spoke at a three-day conference. It was one of my first times being the main speaker instead of one of many speakers. At this particular conference there were also a few workshop teachers who would be offering optional seminars during free time. One of these young women really stuck out to me. Also in her early to mid-twenties, she was very chatty, and we talked a lot throughout the weekend.

I found it very odd that this girl, we'll call her Heather, donned an apron and began cleaning tables and serving food during meal times—after all, there were paid staff to do those things. And at night, after all of the sessions were over, she went around to all of the cabins to stay up chatting with the teen girls to see what they learned, unwittingly stealing the job of their assigned counselors. Quietly I observed all of this without saying a word.

Finally, on the last afternoon, Heather wiped her hands on her apron and plopped down next to me as I was eating lunch. I chose not to broach the subject of my observations, but she volunteered.

"I just never know what is expected of me when they invite me to speak at these things," she said, sighing. "So I usually just grab an apron and join the people in the kitchen or clean tables." I sat there in stunned silence. In an attempt to cover my shock, I chewed on the piece of turkey in my mouth long after it had turned to mush. I think I just nodded and said something profound like "uh-huh" because I didn't feel comfortable sharing what I really wanted to say to her.

If I hadn't been caught so off guard I might have said, "Heather, nobody expects any of this from you. You were invited here to speak—that's exactly what they want you to do. They have kitchen workers and counselors to do the other things. By trying to do everything, you are not only *not* doing what is expected of you, but you are also robbing other people of the opportunity to do what is expected of them." Oh, how I wish I had more courage in moments like that.

Heather's sense of striving to please the conference coordinators stood in stark contrast to another twenty-something I met that weekend. We'll call her Kelly. She was the one who led worship for the conference. As I was packing things up in the back of the chapel one afternoon, I overheard an exchange between Kelly and the wife of one of the men who works at the conference center.

"Have you been invited back for the summer yet?" The woman's voice sounded hopeful as she questioned Kelly.

"Actually, I have been invited to do such-and-such by so-and-so, and to do this and that by another so-and-so," Kelly answered (obviously using real names and events).

"Good." The woman nodded enthusiastically.

"But," Kelly continued, "I have decided just to stay home this summer." The woman's shock was apparent and her response was instant.

"What's wrong?" Her voice was alarmed.

"Nothing's wrong." Kelly carefully went on, "It's just that I have spent the past five summers at camps or out of the country, and I just feel like it's time to take a break."

The woman obviously didn't understand. "Well, hopefully you'll still decide to come up for a few weeks this summer," she said quickly before changing the subject.

How different Kelly's approach to the conference had been to Heather's. Heather came with the intent of covering all of her bases by attempting to fulfill every expectation that anyone *might* have of her with the hope of being invited back. Kelly came and ministered where she knew she was *called* to minister and had been invited back, but knew God was calling her to rest. So risking not receiving a future invitation, she said no.

When I think back on that conference, I try to see where I would place myself. Truthfully, I am probably somewhere between Heather, who has her hand raised desperately searching for permission to just be herself, and Kelly, who is relaxed in who God has made her and doesn't have any regrets about it.

What about you? We all have a tendency to assume others have certain expectations of what our lives should and shouldn't be. And then we try to squeeze ourselves into the mold others have set for us. Sometimes we even do this in the name of nobility or spirituality. Other observers may have thought Heather simply had a servant's heart when she cleaned the kitchen. I only know that wasn't her motivation because she sat down and told me.

What we need to realize is that the approval of other people doesn't always serve as confirmation that we are headed in the right direction. Many times the approval of others stands in stark contrast to the approval of God. (Think about how many times your friends have encouraged you to date the wrong person or pursue the wrong thing.) But it is hard to shake off the sting resulting from a terrible tongue-lashing from someone we respected who is disappointed with our choices.

When Disappointing Others Is the Right Thing to Do

Jesus Christ stands as the perfect example of someone who continually disappointed people in order to please God. The Jews who were looking for a Messiah in Jesus' day were not looking for a Savior who came to establish an eternal kingdom. They were looking for a priestly king who would set up His kingdom right then and there. In John 6:14–15, immediately after Jesus fed the five thousand, the Bible records this incident:

> When the people saw the miraculous sign, they exclaimed, "Surely, he is the Prophet we have been expecting!" Jesus saw that they were ready to take him by force and make him king, so he went higher into the hills alone.

Constantly the crowds and the Pharisees—and in some cases even His disciples—wanted Him to reveal His power and take His earthly kingdom by force. Those who followed Him didn't want a dying and defeated Savior, and those who challenged Him wouldn't believe He was who He claimed to be without a demonstration of evidence. In Matthew 3:17 God's opinion of Jesus is clear: "This is my beloved Son, and I am fully pleased with him." He did not have to perform for God. Neither do we.

For those of us who seek to be Christ followers, boldly living lives that will make a difference, there will be times when we need to part ways with the crowd and their approval. It sounds far easier than it really is. Going without someone's approval isn't like going without lunch—where you'll get a little hungry but can make up for it with dinner. It's much more complex because the absence of approval always means the scornful eye of disapproval.

I (Michael) work in a secular career, and I have first-hand experience watching the disapproval that goes around the office when someone doesn't live up to his or her potential. And as bad as it is to sit in a sales meeting under a manager who is angry at his team, there is something far worse. The disapproval that condescendingly comes from a brother or sister in Christ who is on a self-righteous high leaves a far bloodier wound than any the world can inflict upon us. When another Christian comes to you to launch an outright assault on whether you can or cannot hear the voice of God and apply it, it can have a crippling effect on almost anyone.

> For those of us who seek to be Christ followers, boldly living lives that will make a difference, there will be times when we need to part ways with the crowd and their approval.

In his book *Committed But Flawed*, Cecil Murphey tells of one such incident in his own life:

> *Shirley* [his wife] *and I had been very active in a small but affluent congregation on the north side of Chicago. We felt God call us to serve in Africa, contacted a mission board, were accepted, and began our preparations to leave the country.*
>
> *The pastor of our church—someone I loved dearly—called me on the phone. "This is not God's will," he said.*

For perhaps ten minutes he lectured me, insisting that God had not called us. He never quite said he didn't believe in sending missionaries to other lands, but he did say that national Christians in that country should be held accountable to evangelize and teach their people without any outside "interference."

No matter how carefully I tried to explain our position, my pastor refuted every statement. Finally he said, "We stand against your god on Mount Carmel."

His words shocked me so much that I couldn't believe he had made such a terrible statement.

"What did you say?"

He repeated the statement.

I hung up—I had to because his words hurt so deeply I couldn't speak. He had broken my heart. That was the congregation for whom Shirley and I had worked and served for four years. One summer I had served as the assistant pastor and oversaw all the summer programs. I loved those people, and I felt that we belonged to them and they to us.

I knew what the pastor meant. He referred to the congregation and him as being Elijah on Mount Carmel opposing me, represented by the 450 prophets of Baal. . . . Nothing so far in my Christian experience had crushed me that deeply. Those were my brothers and sisters—individuals and families I had known and loved. The pastor was someone I had loved as if he were my father.

We felt dazed and confused. We did call one woman. "We've been told not to speak to you," she said, "so I don't feel I can disobey." She hung up. We felt more isolated than ever. It hurt to be rejected by our own brothers and sisters in Christ. We continued with our plans because of our absolute certainty of God's will.[1]

[1]Cecil Murphey, *Committed But Flawed* (Chattanooga, TN: Living Ink Books, 2004), 136–137. Used with permission.

Many times that is how it is when we choose to embrace God's will for our lives and leave behind the normal and mundane routines that most people follow. Something in us challenges something in them, and they don't like the challenge so they tell us we are wrong. Or perhaps it is more personal than that. Maybe they are currently getting something from us that they will not continue to get should we actually take a risk and do what we feel called to do.

Other times it boils down to what people think is or isn't fair. In their eyes we shouldn't be able to do what we really want to do if they can't do what they really want to. But what they don't realize is that many times the only one holding them back from pursuing their own dreams is them (and perhaps their own fears).

There will most certainly come a time in all of our lives where obedience to God will require us to disappoint others—sometimes even people we care very deeply about. That is why we chose to include this chapter. When it comes to getting from where you are to where you want to go in life, chances are you will more than likely have to leave behind some (if not all) of the approval you currently have from other people. No one really bothers you when you are safe. They don't challenge you when you are living your life just like everyone else is.

It's when you dare to dream and your movement rocks the boat everyone else was comfortably seated in, that people become disgruntled and even vicious. In that moment you always have two choices—to stay stuck in elementary school, raising your hand and asking for permission before leaving the room, or to accept their venom with grace and confidently move forward knowing you are in the will of God, and that is all that matters.

For most of us, our moments of emancipation come unannounced, when we aren't expecting them. They emerge from one bold decision that leads to another bold decision and eventually turns into a way of life. You must be set free from your addiction for other people's approval before you can truly embrace the life you want to live. The life you want is risky. It's not for the faint of heart. And it most certainly isn't for the approval-addicted. It's for those who know how to say no, who refuse to ask for permission from those with no real authority in their lives, and who do not cower just because someone else has an opinion and decides to be loud about it.

You are on the verge of your emancipation. Step forward with boldness and embrace it—*now*.

FOR FURTHER THOUGHT:

1. Make a list of all of the people you are seeking approval from in your life and how you are seeking their approval. Next, try to determine why their approval is so important to you.

2. Would you classify yourself as someone who can say no confidently or as someone who is always raising a hand to ask for permission? Why is that?

3. Can you recall a time when you lost someone else's approval even though you knew you were doing the right thing? How has that affected you?

4. Does it surprise you that even a godly man like Moses wrestled with whether he would have the approval of men even when he knew he had the approval of God? Why or why not?

5. What percentage of people in your life do you feel know and

accept you for who you really are? Why is that number so high or low?

DO IT NOW

Keep an index card in your purse, pocket, briefcase, or backpack. Make a "T chart" and divide the card into two categories: *Times I Did What I Felt Others Wanted Me To* and *Times I Did What I Really Wanted To Do*. Each time you make a decision—whether it is as simple as going out to dinner or as complicated as choosing a new path in life—mark it in the proper category. At the end of one week, take inventory of how you made your decisions.

❝ *If you always do what you've always done,* **❞**
you'll always be what you've always been.
—Josh McDowell

Home. For most of us that word conjures up warm and fuzzy feelings and, in some cases, a sense of relief. Home—whether it is back in our hometown with our parents, in the sloppy apartment we share with roommates, or in the house or condo we call our very own—is usually one of the only places we don't feel the pressures of the outside world. At home we're allowed to be our true selves. We are surrounded by people who have known us for a long time and don't need explanations for why we are the way we are. At home we feel loved and accepted—or at least we should.

Growing up in a good home can be a breeding ground for success. Living in a safe community where you have the same friends from kindergarten through high school, and where you never have to find a new church because to you church has always been one place and one place only, can breed a sense of security in a person that gives confidence.

Many times this is a false confidence that comes from feeling superior to those around us. If we leave home and venture out, this confidence may quickly dwindle as we realize we aren't as superior as we thought we were. This mentality is often seen on college campuses when the freshmen arrive. Still boasting about being the valedictorian or homecoming queen, they are usually shocked to find that those accomplishments mean nothing outside of the high schools they left behind.

In our travels and in our ministry, Michael and I have met many twentysomethings whose greatest roadblock in getting from where they are to where they want to go in life is simply the comforts and confines of the sense of home they hold on to. For instance, there is the guy in his mid-twenties who has always wanted to go off to college yet has never been able to bring himself to leave his parents' house, so he keeps plugging away at his two part-time dead-end jobs while friend after friend leaves town.

There is also the guy in his late twenties who still lives with his parents and is in a similar situation, only he is working a dead-end full-time job that won't even provide him with enough money to pay bills should he attempt to move out on his own. We have even met a vast influx of young married couples who couldn't handle the financial commitments of being out on their own, so they had to pack their bags and move back home, into the same room one of them grew up in, with their spouse (and sometimes kids) in tow.

I (Shannon) remember hearing the frustrations of a wife in her mid-twenties, with a husband quickly approaching thirty, who was tired and frustrated by living in her in-laws' attic with her young family of four. I also once heard the boastful bragging of a young Christian man living with his in-laws, as he listed off all of the extravagant purchases he and his wife were making since they didn't have a mortgage or other expenses associated with independent life. When he began to complain about a lack of privacy, I stared at him in disbelief.

And I will never forget the young bride I met who was ecstatic that her dad had agreed to pay for everything for her and her new husband, including their wedding bands, their rent, and their college tuition. Throughout the entire conversation I wondered how a person like this could be happy. I mean, who was she married to—her dad or her husband? Finally I realized the concept of *playing* house is appealing to those of us who are afraid to really get out on our own.

Quasi-Independence

Trust me, Michael and I are not against getting help from your parents in the transition from young adulthood to full-blown adulthood. We both lived at home in the last year or so before our wedding in an attempt to save money. By the time we got married, both our cars were paid off and we had several thousand dollars in the bank—neither of which would have been possible had each of us lived on our own. We were also able to take cash with us on our honeymoon so we didn't go into debt just so we could go where we wanted to go. Not having many bills to pay during that time helped us get ahead in ways we are extremely grateful for and will never forget. But we have also seen more than a handful of twentysomethings take advantage of this system to their own detriment.

Quasi-independence is not real independence, and you do yourself a great disservice when you try to pretend it is. Instead of being like the young man who lived with his in-laws and blew every dime he brought in, those of us who live at home in our twenties need to use the generosity of our parents as a chance to get ahead. Otherwise we will be dependent upon living with our parents (or off of their resources) for the rest of our lives.

I remember being in college and receiving two pieces of invaluable advice from other twentysomethings who had moved back home after graduation. They were easy to remember, and I applied them both. The first piece of advice was to have a set time for leaving—have a goal and stick to it. I have friends who decided that after college graduation they were packing up their childhood rooms and never moving home again. Others I know moved home for a year, or while they had to hold down an unpaid internship like student teaching. And some, like me, moved back home for the brief window between college graduation and their wedding.

My goal started at the one-year mark—I was moving home for one year after college. But in that year I got engaged, and as my parents and I talked about it, we thought it was in my best interest to bump my deadline back a bit and have me stay for the remaining handful of months until my wedding. It's okay to adjust your goal once or twice as new developments arise. You cannot expect to have the next five years of your life figured out at any point in your twenties—it's too tumultuous of a decade. Things change really fast. If you extend your deadline more than twice, though, you run the risk of being one of those twentysomethings who never leaves.

Michael and I met a Christian woman who was trying hard to teach her young adult son responsibility—so she charged him rent. What he didn't know was that, on the day he moved out, she was going to return every last dime to him as a gift. Some parents may seem hard-nosed when it comes to how they do and don't help

> *You cannot expect to have the next five years of your life figured out at any point in your twenties—it's too tumultuous of a decade. Things change really fast.*

their adult children. More times than not, though, they have the best interest of their child at heart. So if your parents kick you out or charge you rent, know that they are doing it because they want to teach you to thrive and not to take a free handout just because you can.

The other piece of advice I was given was to save as much money as possible during the months I lived with my parents after graduation. In addition to writing full-time during that phase of my life, I also held down a part-time job at my church. As I worked on three books I was writing for my publisher, I taught the principles I was writing about to teen girls in my church each week. I decided to save all of my writing income and live exclusively off of what I made at church (which wasn't much). But for me, it worked. And by the time Michael and I got married, we were able to pay off any remaining debts and have a solid nest egg in our savings account.

If you are living with your parents or are contemplating doing so again, use the opportunity as a stepping-stone to thrust you forward—it can be a great tool in catapulting you toward some of your goals a lot more rapidly. Don't let your parents' generosity become a roadblock that prevents you from moving forward at all.

In our research for this book, Michael and I have learned that financial pressures and parents' generosity aren't the only things that keep twentysomethings tied to home. Often there are two other factors that keep them stuck where they are instead of getting them where they want to go: Familiar people and the only way of life they have ever known.

Where Everybody Knows Your Name

Shannon and I (Michael) both grew up in churches where we had the same group of friends from Sunday school through youth group. Every church memory we have has the same people in it, give or take a few. There was a great sense of comfort that came from being part of the group—you have a lot of common history with people, and some of those things can bond you to people for life. But sometimes that common history also destines you to have a common future with these very same people even if the future they want is not the future *you* want for yourself.

When I was just out of high school, my two best friends at the time were both in serious relationships with the girls they would end up marrying. Being single can be viewed as taboo in the Christian community if you stay single for too long—especially in a small town where almost everyone is married before the age of twenty-five. And I didn't want to be the last man standing. So when a nice enough girl came along and showed interest in me, I jumped head-first into a relationship that never should have been as serious as it was, and honestly never should have happened at all, solely because I didn't want to be the last man standing. I ruined and wasted a good few years of my life and nearly ruined my future just because I wanted my life to keep pace with the lives of the others who were part of my group. Oddly enough, it was that same mistake that ultimately led to the unraveling of my friendship with the same group I wanted to keep pace with.

Sometimes it can be hard to move past your mistakes when you remain friends with people who will never let you forget them. When something happens in your life that marks you, those people will keep pointing out that mark to every new person you meet. Any person who joins the circle you have always been part of will quickly hear all the garbage the rest of you have been through, because it inevitably becomes part of the "remember when" conversations that mark friendships rooted in the past, not in the present.

It is very easy for a person who spends his or her life as part of a group to lose any sense of his or her true identity. In a group, you are part of a whole, and you are not whole yourself. Every decision you make becomes exactly like the one everyone else in the group would make if they were faced with your situation.

Recently, in a conversation with someone from our

hometown, Shannon asked about what had happened to a certain guy we all knew. "I don't know," our friend quickly said. "He joined a band and is touring right now or something." The comment passed and the conversation went on. But when we got back in the car, Shannon jumped immediately back to that point in the conversation.

"Did you hear the tone with which that statement was said?" She crossed her arms and looked at me in disbelief.

"Not really," I answered as I kept my eyes focused on the road, trying to avoid the fire I could see brewing in her eyes.

"They said he joined a band and left town like it was a bad thing. And what, staying here forever is supposed to be good for everyone?" Her tone continued to rise as she spoke. For the next twenty minutes she proceeded to explain why that type of mentality ruined people. Her points were valid. Sometimes sticking with familiar people, and their familiar ways, can be the worst decision you could ever make for yourself. Sometimes moving on, or pursuing a dream no one else really agrees with, is the best option. But you cannot always expect others to go with you on your journey.

In his book *Yes, You Can!* Art Linkletter tells a story about a friend who purchased over a hundred acres of land in the middle of nowhere with the goal of building a place where families could go on vacation. There would be rides and restaurants and all sorts of things families could do together. Mr. Linkletter's friend had made a significant investment in this place he was going to call "Disney-land,"and he invited Mr. Linkletter to buy the surrounding land to build hotels on. Mr. Linkletter, thinking his friend was crazy, turned down the offer. *Who in the world is going to drive twenty-five miles to ride a roller coaster?* he wondered. Later, Mr. Linkletter remembered his long walk back to the car that day, because he figures it cost him about one million dollars per step.[1]

Art Linkletter and Walt Disney never let this difference in opinions come between their friendship. Any friend worth keeping won't let your desire to pursue your dream get in the way of your friendship.

> *Any friend worth keeping won't let your desire to pursue your dream get in the way of your friendship.*

When we first started dating, I found it quite baffling when Shannon told me some of her best friends were girls she saw only several times a year. Their lives had taken them in completely different directions, but they still loved, supported, and prayed for one another the same. We now spend our summers flying to visit some of these friends or we have them out to visit us. I can see now that those girls are some of the best friends Shannon could ever ask for. A true friend is a rare find because he or she is willing to let you go (and sacrifice a daily relationship with you) in order to let you chase your dreams and pursue God's will for your life.

---

[1]Art Linkletter, *Yes, You Can!* (New York: Simon and Schuster, 1979), 247–248.

John Maxwell wrote:

> *As you seek to enlist people into the fulfillment of your vision, don't be discouraged when people can't see what you do. And don't despair if people you respect won't take the trip with you—even if you're inviting them to do it for their own benefit. Celebrate when people choose to join you. And keep loving those who don't.*[2]

Making new friends when you venture out to pursue what it is you really want to do can be tough. Shannon remembers venturing off to college knowing only one girl there. Coming out of college she had a handful of lifelong best friends and had lost touch with that girl she knew in the beginning.

During my last semester of Bible college I studied abroad in Israel. I left the United States not knowing a soul who would be studying with me in that time. By the end of the semester I had found a good friend in my roommate Keyan. He later was a groomsman in my wedding, and we still continue to meet for coffee every Thursday morning, years after returning back home.

Most of us can remember back to a time when we didn't know the friends we have today. They were strangers to us once too. Getting to know them was awkward and forced, and then one day something just clicked and we have been close ever since. There are new friends waiting to be made in the life that is waiting to be lived. Take the risk and step out with or without the approval of the friends you have today.

---

[2]John Maxwell, *The Journey From Success to Significance* (Nashville: J Countryman, 2004), 94.

Same Old, Same Old

People aren't the only thing we grow accustomed to when we make ourselves comfortable back at home. A certain way of life is something we learn early on, and we are not quick to abandon it. This is why Christians who were raised in the church sometimes have a hard time relating to people who don't believe in God or don't believe Jesus is who He says He is. Those who never lived without knowledge of God just can't imagine what it is like.

The same is true with other beliefs and convictions people hold. When Shannon and I were engaged we sought the counsel of several godly couples we admired and respected. One couple that gave us a lot of insight into the world of marriage really surprised us. The wife, who had given advice to a lot of brides over the years, said she had never counseled a couple where the wife also had a career. In the beginning of our time with this couple, Shannon really felt as if her career was a roadblock this woman wasn't going to be able to move past. Eventually she did, but only after making a few comments that Shannon interpreted as jabs at women who had careers. Shannon was able to put her hurt feelings aside and glean a lot from this woman, but in the beginning their different experiences made it difficult for them to see eye-to-eye.

We recently had some friends from our old church visit our new church with us. The church we attended in our smaller town has roughly three thousand members and is considered huge where it is located. Our new church, which is smack in the middle of hustle-bustle Orange

County, has roughly ten thousand members.

As Shannon was sitting with our friends in our church's café after the service, the wife looked around the café and sprawling bookstore and finally said, "I wonder what God thinks of all of this." Her tone was sharp.

"What do you mean?" Shannon asked, suppressing a smile. She had already shared with me that she thought this particular friend was having a hard time with some of the differences between our old church and our new one.

"Well, the Bible talks about the den of thieves and stuff," she said, still eyeing the impressive room she was sitting in.

"I don't think God has a problem with any of it," Shannon said calmly. "Especially since all proceeds from the café and bookstore go to global missions." Stunned, our friend's eyes grew big as she asked for proof on a sign or something. When she made a purchase later that afternoon, it said "All proceeds go to global outreach" right on her bag. Later, Shannon chuckled to herself when she overheard that same friend telling another friend (who wasn't there) how great it is that our church gives to missions in that way.

Sometimes people get so tied to their idea of normal that they cannot see past differences that could possibly lead them into a change that is right. Most people shy away from change. But you do not grow if you do not change. No one has it all figured out right where they are. There are new things all of us could afford to learn, things we would all grow from if we implemented them.

Shannon and I haven't always lived in Orange County. We haven't always attended the church we are members of now. We moved here when we first got married—we left the town where we both grew up and moved to this place where we knew essentially no one. And after months and months of church hopping—and trying to find a place where we fit—we finally found our new church home. We are still awkwardly stumbling through the initial stages of new friendships. We are adapting to a new way of life. We are changing and growing—and we are thriving. We absolutely love it here. And when people ask if we ever miss the town we moved from, our answer is an honest no. But it wasn't always that way. It took time.

One thing it took us a while to learn was that, when you leave the comforts of your current home behind in an attempt to get from where you are to where you want to go in life, there is a new home with new comforts waiting for you wherever you choose to settle. It may not feel just like the home you came from. There will more than likely be some adjustments you need to make as you experience some growing pains. You may need to alter your expectations a little, and it may make you more than a little uncomfortable in the beginning. At moments you may wish you could pack your bags and head back to where you came from.

But some forms of growth come only from taking risks and making changes. Look at it this way: The home you are so comfortable in now (whether "home" means your living situation, the friends you are surrounded by, or the way of life you have been conditioned to think is normal) has left you wanting. Something in your soul is crying out for something more. That's why you are reading a book on getting from where you are to where you want to go. Every journey involves putting one foot in front of the other and moving forward. In order to move forward, you must leave something behind.

Your moment has come. It's time to get just a little bit uncomfortable. And it's time to do it *now*. What are you waiting for?

FOR FURTHER THOUGHT:

1. Do you currently have a plan in place to gain complete independence from your parents? If yes, what is it? If no, why not?

2. Do you have friends or family members who constantly remind you of past mistakes? If so, how does it make you feel? Do you currently remind others of their past mistakes? If so, why?

3. What are you looking for in your friendships at this point in your life?

4. Have you ever tried to help a friend move forward just to have him or her tell you that he or she wasn't interested? If so, how did it affect your relationship and your ability to achieve your own goals?

5. Does the life you envision having ten years from now look just like the life you (and others around you) had growing up? Walk yourself through the similarities and differences (e.g., I will live in a neighborhood much like the one I grew up in, or I will leave my small town and move to a big city, etc.).

DO IT NOW

Pull out a map and make a list of three to five new cities you would consider moving to (in a dream world, if you aren't ready to contemplate moving in reality). Go online and research those cities and write a one-page (or more) story about what your life could be like if you moved to those cities and began pursuing your dreams. For instance, musicians might consider Nashville, and aspiring actors might consider Los Angeles or New York City. Don't hold back— dream big and let your imagination run wild.

> **"** *There are risks and costs to a program of action.* **"**
> *But they are far less than the long-range risks*
> *and costs of comfortable inaction.*
> *—John F. Kennedy*

Somewhere at the end of my (Shannon's) *early* twenties, just as I was getting ready to cross the threshold into my *mid*-twenties, I stumbled upon what I consider to be a very profound truth. Tired and weary from months of constant traveling and speaking, and a bit burned out from writing so many books in such a short period of time, I realized that I had become rather halfhearted in my approach to most things.

Sure, I always gave *what I could* to each project I set out to tackle. But there was a certain element missing— *excellence.* Somewhere along the line I had lowered the bar for myself so that I could keep going without stopping in my tired and weary existence. It was as if I were running a race I no longer intended to win. Appalled at what I discovered, I seriously contemplated giving up entirely and just dropping out of the race. I'm not talking about ending my life. I'm talking about giving up on my dreams— which, in a way, would have killed the most alive part of me.

So with deadlines looming and events that were booked long ago quickly approaching, I just stopped—okay, I got laryngitis and I was forced to stop—and I took some time to reevaluate this lack of enthusiasm for life that I was experiencing. And slowly, as if I were emerging from a fog, the truth began to become clear to me. *In order to give my best to something, I had to be at my best.* Tired, frazzled, and carrying a few extra pounds, I was not at my best—and that explained my halfhearted effort toward everything I did. Living at my best would have included more energy and less weight. It would mean living with a passion that would automatically infuse everything I did.

> Each of us was made to be nothing short of extraordinary.

Subconsciously I had gotten so busy trying to be *the* best—and failing—that I no longer had the energy to be *my* best. If you ever want to get from where you are to where you want to go in life, you must get to a place where you are no longer satisfied with halfhearted living. You have to learn that even if everyone else does something a certain way, if you aren't satisfied, or you aren't giving your all, then you are selling yourself short. Being normal and average is settling. I'm not talking about your career choice here. I'm talking about living a life of impact versus a life that doesn't make a difference. The truth is each of us was made to be nothing short of extraordinary.

For me, abandoning average to get to excellent came through taking six steps toward a major lifestyle change. Even though we are all at different places in life and we have different goals in mind, these six steps are applicable to all of us no matter where we are on our journey. They can help us abandon average and get to excellent. As long as we decide that being *the* best is not as important as being *our* best, these principles can really work for us. You might not be able to win the Olympic gold, but you shouldn't let that hinder you from achieving your goal of running in the Boston Marathon.

Principle #1: Never Stop Learning

By the time I hit my crisis point, I already had my bachelor's degree and saw no need to go into debt for a master's, considering it wouldn't further my career. But that didn't give me an excuse to stop being a student. Shortly into my epiphany about excellence, I realized that I had been so busy writing books and speaking at conferences that I had stopped *reading* books and *attending* conferences. There just wasn't enough time to do everything, or so I claimed. And you know what? I didn't improve as a writer or a speaker during that time. Subconsciously I chose to stop learning.

Deciding that this horrible pattern had to go, I quickly devoured several books on the bestseller lists and a handful of books by some of my author friends. I registered myself for a women's conference and a marriage conference with Michael, and I sat in on workshops offered by other speakers at conferences where I was also speaking.

Every time I put a book down or left a seminar, I felt as if I had been enlightened by the content. It was only after I sat down to write or prepare to speak that I began to notice that I had also picked up several new techniques when it came to delivery. And the strangest thing happened—people began to notice a change in my writing and speaking.

"You've blown any event I ever attended out of the water," one woman said to me recently at the close of a conference where I spoke. I smiled politely and thanked her, knowing that I owed all of the credit to the Lord and the long list of writers and speakers who had just unknowingly mentored me through their work.

Immediately after I opened my mind and heart back up to learning, a change began to take place in me. Without even realizing it, I began to get rid of my own bad habits and imitate the best in others. By choosing to make time to learn from others, I found myself returning to the place I classified as *my* best.

No matter how busy you are, and whether you are a current student or a recent grad, you need to make time to learn about the things that interest you in life. Whether your focus is spiritual growth, professional growth, or personal growth, it is vital that you take the time to listen to what others have to say and study topics that will be helpful to you in your relationships, your career, your goals, and your life. In order to get from where you are to where you want to go, you will need to learn and grow along the way. You don't currently have everything you need to get there. If you did, you would be there already.

Principle #2: Take Care of Your Body and It Will Take Care of You

The Bible clearly states in 1 Corinthians 6:19 that our bodies are the temple of the Holy Spirit. But honestly, I never paid much attention to that. For the first two decades of my life, I was blessed with a good metabolism. As my mom claims, I wouldn't even say the word exercise, much less actually do it. Sure, I played some sports growing up. And I was the second worst person on my softball team. I say second worst because there was one girl who somehow always managed to trip over first base and wind up sprawled out several feet away, where the other team could easily tag her out. She was the *only* one on the team who was worse than me. What does that tell you about my athletic abilities?

But at the time I began to experience my quarter-life crisis, I was tired, carrying a few extra pounds, and just plain sluggish. I wasn't happy with how I looked, and I wasn't happy with how I felt. And it was evident in everything I did. In fact, it was often the first thought in my mind when I woke up in the morning. So on the horrifying evening that I discovered I was no longer living at my best, I made a firm decision. I was going to change both my eating habits and my (lack of) exercise habits.

I knew I needed something extreme. So I got a personal trainer and started doing Pilates on reformer machines twice a week. A few weeks into it, I added a class. Then I introduced two days of at-home sessions on my own. Within one month results were obvious—I was down two, and in some cases three, pant sizes. I had more energy. I felt good, and I felt like I looked good.

At the same time I began exercising, I also changed my diet. People began talking with me about what types of foods my blood type needed and the differences between good fats and carbs and bad fats and carbs. I didn't go on a diet. Rather, I changed the way I cooked and ate—even while traveling—and this too contributed to my higher energy and slimmer figure. In fact, I worked so hard in these two areas that I quickly dropped down to a size smaller than I was on my wedding day (for all of you male readers, this is a big deal in a woman's eyes). I even built muscle tone.

Although it could have been easy to compare myself to the other women who came into the Pilates studio, or to the slender and sleek frame of my trainer, I reminded myself that I wasn't there to compete with them. I was there to compete with myself. The only person I needed to best was the tired, sluggish, and somewhat chubby version of me that first walked into the studio.

The thing that really motivated me to change in this area was the realization that even if I achieved all of my other life goals, I would still be perpetually unhappy because of the way I felt and the way I saw myself. What difference does success and achievement make if you feel fat, ugly, and burned out?

The key to finding freedom in this area comes from acknowledging that diet and exercise is not a worldwide contest. You are not competing against everyone else out there. If you view your eating and exercise habits this way, you can quickly find yourself in unhealthy bondage in the form of an eating disorder or exercise obsession. If this is something you struggle with, get accountability and maybe even professional assistance in the form of a personal trainer, nutritionist, or doctor before making any changes to your normal routine.

In order to be your best, the only person you need to compete with is yourself. Find your target weight or size (and don't measure it against other people's target weight or size) and work toward that goal. Having more energy and feeling better about how you look (for women this could be a matter of a slimmer, trimmer figure whereas for men this could be a matter of a more muscular physique) will enable you to reach all of your other goals far more quickly. Ever since I made changes in these areas of my own life, I have found that I am far more productive on a daily basis and that I am more adventurous in my approach to life.

Making changes in this, and any, area of your life requires a good mix of discipline and patience. Results do not always occur overnight, and sometimes we make mistakes and take a few steps backward before righting ourselves again. Do not get discouraged. It is possible for God to give you a permanent motivation to make changes in this area. If God could do it for me, He most certainly can do it for you. For some ideas on how to help you get started in this area, please look at the appendix or visit our Web site for a more exhaustive list of suggestions.

Principle #3: Remove the Clutter

Christian personality John Tesh has a late-night radio program on our local Christian radio station. Michael listens to it far more than I do because he is in the car a lot for work, but every time I have listened I have taken away at least one action point from his "advice for life" segment. (You can glean some of his advice by visiting *www.tesh.com*).

On one particular night, during this crisis time in my life, John mentioned something about a study that proved people who were surrounded by less clutter and more order proved to be several times more productive than people who were surrounded by more clutter. Anyone who knows me knows that clutter is my middle name. My desk almost always looks like a hurricane has hit it—even when the rest of my home is immaculate.

So, much to Michael's delight, I chose to implement John Tesh's strategy in my own life and see how it worked out. One day after Michael left for his office, I went into our home office with a trash can and began sorting through everything that didn't have a proper home. After filing certain things where they belonged and evaluating if other items were really worth keeping, I threw away lots of stuff. My trash can was overflowing by the time I was through. Just cleaning up my clutter made me feel as if I had accomplished something huge; I couldn't imagine what it would do to my daily productivity.

Sure enough, John Tesh was right. Shortly after my cleaning binge, I found myself accomplishing my to-do list in one day rather than the full week it had taken me before. Think about your desk, cubicle, car, or area where you spend most of your time. Are there unnecessary papers, magazines, and pictures piling up? Do you often find yourself overwhelmed by the simple sight of this specific area? Maybe for you your clutter isn't even noticeable anymore because you have gotten so used to it. So the simple inclination that you aren't as productive as you would like to be might be your warning light to begin noticing your clutter once again—and to eliminate it for good.

All of us could afford to un-clutter our lives, at least a little. Chances are, if we want to get from where we are to where we want to go in life (and do it *now*), we are going to need to maximize our productivity and make the most of our time. Un-cluttering your life will help accelerate your progress on your journey toward your goals.

Principle #4: Clearly Outline Your Goals and Put Them Where You Will See Them

Just before reaching my crisis point, I received a Christmas gift that would help me immensely on the journey toward progress that I didn't realize I was about to begin. It was a Bible study targeted at helping you determine your life goals.[1] During the course of the ten weeks, there was assigned reading, an audio message, and some short-answer reflection questions. And then a huge component designed to help you map out—and achieve—your goals.

The Bible study came with flash cards divided into categories: spiritual, relational, physical, financial, career, etc. On each card you had to write one overriding goal and several mini-goals to help you get there. Then you were supposed to keep your flash cards in a place you would see them often (your car, your desk, etc.) and review them frequently. At some points the Bible study even suggested using a personal photo or a magazine cutout to help remind you of your goals. For instance, if you have vacationed in Hawaii and desperately want to return, tuck a photo from your previous trip next to your ATM card in your wallet to remind you to choose wisely before spending.

I have always been a highly motivated person—I graduated from college in three and a half years and started my career before I even graduated. Having goals is ingrained in my DNA. But I cannot tell you how much clearer—and more reachable—my goals became once I began to write

---

[1]Blueprint for Life *www.blueprintforlife.com*, 2005.

them down and consciously run them through my mind on a regular basis. My daily actions eventually began to be weighed against my future goals—*Do I really want to do this now if it means getting me off track from getting that then?* As I did this, I discovered, perhaps for the first time, what I really wanted out of life, and I gained a pretty good idea of whether my current path would help me get there.

An excerpt from the *Blueprint for Life* workbook says:

> It's estimated that only three percent of the population has ever bothered to write down their goals. . . . When it comes right down to it, most of us don't want to take the chance of facing disappointment when things don't turn out like we planned. It's much safer just to keep our ambitions tucked safely in the back of our minds somewhere— quietly dreaming, but never boldly reaching. After all, nobody wants to be wrong on paper. . . . Living by goals means making sacrifices, being self-disciplined, and denying ourselves the freedom to go with the flow.[2]

Oddly enough, writing down my goals and regularly reviewing them helped me make more progress than any other method I have ever tried. It helped me keep the things I wanted to do most—the things I felt the Lord leading me to do with my life—at the forefront of my mind. And it eliminated my desire to drag my feet in doing those things.

A man by the name of Robert Heinlein once said, "In the absence of clearly defined goals, we become strangely loyal to performing daily trivia until ultimately we become enslaved by it." If we do not put our goals on paper, it is

---

[2]Blueprint for Life.

far too easy to live a normal and average life in mediocrity and closet disappointment.

What about you? Have you ever written your goals down on paper? It might be time to grab a stack of three-by-five cards and start making your own set of flash cards that will help you abandon average and get to excellent rather quickly.

Principle #5: Celebrate Your Progress

One thing Shannon and I (Michael) have made a habit of doing is celebrating our progress. Every time we reach even the minutest of milestones on our checklist of progress, we celebrate. It's not always something extravagant like a vacation or a new car, but it is something out of the ordinary like a dinner out at a fancy place or a trip to the store to purchase something small we have been wanting like a new CD or DVD. Other times we celebrate by getting together with friends. We have learned that celebration keeps you going even when you feel as if you aren't making as much progress at the moment as you would like to.

Every time Shannon is offered a new book contract, we celebrate. Every time I win a contest or get a bonus at work, we celebrate. Every time we have reached a financial goal—like saving for something specific—we celebrate. Just recently we discovered that we were on target to save several thousand dollars more than we had set out to save this year. It still wasn't enough for a down payment on a house in the neighborhood we want to move to, but it got us several steps closer to our ultimate goal—so we celebrated.

When was the last time you celebrated your own progress, even if what you accomplished didn't seem like that big of a deal to anyone else? We cannot measure our success or our goals against anyone else's success or goals. It's too easy to get off track and become consumed with being the best and becoming discouraged when we fail. Instead we need to focus our time and efforts on being our best and maximizing the potential and resources God has given us exclusively.

Henry David Thoreau once said, "Why should we be in such desperate haste to succeed, and in such desperate enterprises? If a man does not keep pace with his companions, perhaps it is because he hears a different drummer. Let him step to the music which he hears, however measured or far away. It is not important that he should mature as soon as an apple tree or an oak."[3]

Focus on celebrating *your* progress and moving toward *your* goals. Follow the dream God has placed in *your* heart. And work at living life at *your* best—leave the pressure of being *the* best up to someone else.

Principle #6: Spend Time With God

When Shannon came down with laryngitis right in the middle of this crisis point in her life, she was scheduled to be the main speaker at a girls' conference three days later. The doctor ordered her to twenty-four hours of complete silence. This was not easy for someone as verbal as Shannon. Had I been ordered to such a period of silence, it may have been easier for me to concede. But because of Shannon's state of weariness, she was able to oblige her doctor without protesting. She propped herself up in our bed with the bed-

---

[3]Henry David Thoreau, *Walden* (Boston: Ticknor and Fields, 1854).

room door shut and spent the entire day in silence alone with God.

When I came in to check on her after being at work for several hours, I noticed an instant change in the appearance of her face. She looked freer and less weary than she had in months. I'll let her explain:

Michael's right. My forced day of silence taught me a lesson I had failed to learn in the previous twenty-some years of my life. A born talker, I spend much of my personal time with the Lord in prayer or writing in my journal. Rarely am I silent enough to let Him get a word in edgewise. Sure, I listen for the voice of the Lord, but when you consider the percentage of time I spend *speaking* to Him, I don't take nearly enough time to *listen* to Him. At least I didn't before my bout with laryngitis.

I learned more in that one day of silence than I had in the entire six months prior. So I decided to make silence a discipline in my busy life. Now I designate one day each month to be my silent day with God. For eight entire hours I abandon my cell phone, e-mail, music, and anything else that might distract me, and I get alone with the Lord and listen. Sometimes I read the Bible or a book on spiritual growth He has led me to. Usually I spend a portion of my day writing in my journal (but I don't let this be the bulk of my time, since in journaling I am the one doing all the talking). And I pray—but I practice the new element of listening for His replies to my heart's cries.

I emerge from these days with a lighter soul—as if my heavy, well-worn soul has been aired out and refreshed for future use. Now when the weeks have dragged on and my day of silence is approaching, I find myself counting the hours until I can shut everything else away and spend time in absolute silence with the Lord. One friend of mine decided she was going to put her own spin on this practice and implement one hour of silence every day for forty days. She emerged from her experience claiming what I had—she had never learned as much about God as she did when she was silent with Him.

Silence isn't a much practiced discipline these days. We live in a society full of noise. Recently I (Michael) decided that I was going to give up my hours of listening to ESPN sports radio while I was driving to and from appointments, and that I was going to replace that program with Scripture memory. Using flash cards to aid me, I would read and repeat the verses aloud to myself as I drove, and by the time I got home I would sometimes have several multi-verse passages memorized. Shannon was shocked by how quickly I abandoned the radio, since I don't do well without outside noise.

Giving up several hours of radio time has been a huge sacrifice for me, but the tradeoff for what I am getting instead—a wealth of Bible knowledge—is definitely worth it. As Christian men and women, our lives are about giving God glory. But most of us settle for church on Sunday mornings and maybe attending a small group in the middle of the week. We don't take it much further than that.

Really, God is the only One who can take our lives from normal and average to excellent and extraordinary. And He is the One with the best plan for getting us from where we are to where He wants us to go (which may or may not be where we want to go—more on that later in the book). So it is vitally important to tune in to His voice and take time to listen. If we don't, we might miss something. And sometimes the pieces we miss are important and could prevent us from serious heartache if only we would take the time to hear them and heed them.

> God is the only One who can take our lives from normal and average to excellent and extraordinary.

There is something seemingly unfinished about a normal life. It's just so boring, so mundane. So ordinary and average. Anyone can be average. But not anyone can be you. So be the best you that you can be, and raise the bar to a higher standard of living. Be you. Be true. Be excellent.

FOR FURTHER THOUGHT:

1. Are a healthy diet and regular exercise part of your weekly routine? If yes, how does that help motivate you to reach your other goals? If not, how are you being affected negatively by your lack of discipline in this area?

2. Explain how the concept of being *your* best, instead of being *the* best, can bring you freedom.

3. How have you noticed that clutter (or a lack thereof) affects your productivity?

4. Why do you think celebrating the little things keeps us motivated to do the big things?

5. In your time alone with God, do you tend to talk more than you listen? If so, how can you go about changing that?

DO IT NOW

Find a photograph or picture from a magazine that represents a goal you have in your life (remember the Hawaii photo by the ATM card?) and stick it somewhere relevant. Leave it there for a few weeks and see if the photo helps motivate you toward your goal.

" *Everyone thinks of changing the world,* **"**
but no one thinks of changing himself.
—Leo Tolstoy

Let's be honest. We like to be in control. I (Shannon) honestly don't know a person who doesn't. Perhaps one of the biggest differences between *dreaming* our dreams and *pursuing* our dreams is control—when we are still dreaming we are in control, we can make things play out in our minds any way we want to. We can create a whole world of make-believe in our minds and take it to such an extreme that we aren't even living in reality anymore. When we stop dreaming and begin pursuing, there is a significant chance that something might not go according to our plan and we might have to face some disappointments along the way. Haven't you heard the saying *Things aren't always quite how you play them out in your head?* That's a true statement—especially with something as big and important as our deepest passions and wildest dreams.

It seems as if recently we have met a vast influx of young people who are finding that things aren't quite how they played them out in their minds. For instance, there was the young woman who graduated from college with over forty thousand dollars in credit card debt and student loans. Her plan had always been to venture onto the mission field after college, but sadly, she found that most missions organizations won't accept someone with such a weighty debt load for fear that she won't be able to repay her debts while living off of support.

So as the months go by, she keeps making her minimum payments because it is all she can afford, and the years pass without the realization of her dream. While she was still dreaming, those around her told her that a solid education would be a great asset to a missionary—no one seemed to mention that her debt would keep her from ever getting to the mission field in the first place. While she was still dreaming, she felt in control—like she had a plan. Once she started pursuing, her efforts fell flat. Now she is faced with the unexpected question, "What am I supposed to do with my life?"

We also met a woman who was devastated when a dating relationship that lasted almost five years ended in a breakup. Her friends were getting married and starting families, and she was left all alone thinking, *This isn't how it played out in my head.* There were many unexpected lonely nights and weddings she had to attend without a date. Many times she looked at her married friends and thought, *That should have been me.*

Another woman we met found the love of her life and started down the path to happily ever after only to find that, when the time came, she and her husband could not have any children. After months and years of trying to get pregnant, they were told it was never going to happen. "That's not what you expect to hear," she told me sadly. "You don't think you are going to find the person you want to spend the rest of your life with and settle down only to discover that you can never have your own family. That's just not in your plan." Things didn't unfold for her the way she thought they would.

After sitting with people and listening to their agonizing stories, we came to the realization that many times there is something deeper going on in the face of these disappointments than most people realize. Deep beneath the surface, where it goes almost unnoticed, a spirit of anger is beginning to set in. Twentysomethings everywhere are becoming disgruntled, upset, and angry at the way their lives are taking shape. They want to be in control, and they aren't. And when things don't play out like they always imagined they would, a slow and steady rage begins to boil beneath the surface until one day it explodes into the angry realization that life is not fair.

While it is perfectly normal to become upset when things don't happen like you think they should, it is very important that you begin to identify your true feelings before anger takes over and puts down permanent roots in your life. Many people choose to live in anger. Take, for instance, this classified:

Wedding dress for sale. Never worn. Will trade for .38 caliber pistol.[1]

Have you ever met an angry person? You can usually recognize them right away. They usually have a scowl on their face and an "I hate the world" mentality. "Tough," they say to others when their dreams fall apart. "Life's not

---

[1] Charles Stanley, *The Tale of the Tardy Ox Cart* (Nashville: Word, 1998), 33.

fair." With no sense of compassion, and with a hardness of spirit, they make their way through life feeling ripped off and entitled to make others feel the same way.

The best solution to resolving anger that I have ever heard came through a sermon taught by Pastor Kenton Beshore. In that sermon he gave me a tool that has since sounded a warning bell in my mind every time I even begin to get angry about something.

Find a Feeling

Kenton said that when something begins to bother us, we need to learn to identify why it bothers us. He calls it "finding a feeling." "When you get upset, if you don't find a feeling, there is a feeling that will always find you," he said, "and that feeling is anger."[2] From there he began to unpack a list of feelings we may really be experiencing but aren't identifying.

For instance, let's revisit the three women we used in analogies earlier. The woman who wanted to venture onto the mission field might find herself getting angry at others—and even at God—if she doesn't identify the fact that what she really feels is helpless and cheated. She had a big plan—one for God's glory even—and there is nothing she can do to make this plan happen even though all she heard about for four years was what an excellent missionary she would make.

The young woman who endured the breakup might get angry at men or happy couples if she is not able to get

---

[2]Kenton Beshore, *Life Investments,* originally taught on October 2, 2005, as part of the *A Father's Wisdom* series. For DVD and CD ordering info please visit *www.marinerschurch.org.*

a handle on the fact that she feels rejected by her ex-boyfriend and fearful that she may never get married. After nearly five years in a dead-end relationship, she feels as if she is running out of time.

The woman who cannot have her own children may become easily angered if she doesn't acknowledge that she feels like less of a woman because she cannot bear children. Ever since childhood she has been taught to play house, and now she will never have a home quite like the one she imagined.

Anger can easily rile men when they lose in sports and feel as if their best wasn't good enough when their manhood was on the line.

In his sermon, Kenton also mentioned that anger isn't what you are really feeling but is merely an indicator that there is more going on than you realize. Anger is what we get when we don't really deal with our emotions. Ever since hearing that sermon, I can hear his voice warning me, "Find a feeling. Come on now, find a feeling. Hurry up and find a feeling," as I get closer and closer to giving in to anger. And every time I heed that warning and find and identify what my real feelings are, the anger that is rising inside of me subsides and I am able to handle life's disappointments with much more grace. One couple in our small group told us they actually say the phrase "find a feeling" to each other when they feel a marital conflict coming on.

Disappointment is a very real part of life. There will

> *Anger is what we get when we don't really deal with our emotions.*

be moments when you are hurt and let down. And no matter how badly you want to be in control, there will be moments where you simply aren't. And there will be nothing you can do about it. Those are the moments when you will need to find a feeling. Even when life seems as if it is spinning out of control, we need to be reminded that there is always one area where we *can* maintain a sense of control: ourselves.

Self-Control: The Key to a Fruitful Life

Galatians 5:23 tells us that the fruit of the Spirit is self-control. I (Michael) hate the concept of having to work on self-control. I would much rather be out of control when I want to be. Sometimes it seems like self-control requires too much discipline. When you are working really hard to get to a goal but everything unexpectedly falls apart at the end, self-control is needed. All your hard work—and all your sacrifices—seems to have been in vain. What you want to do is blow up at the world, and maybe even blow up at God. But you are told that the right thing to do is take it in stride and act like nothing is bothering you. Sometimes this can upset you even more, and understandably so.

But I think that somewhere along the way we have gotten it wrong. Self-control doesn't mean that life's disappointments and setbacks don't bother us—it means that they no longer cause us to act out. Instead of responding to bad news and being controlled by it, we begin to accept it from the hand of God as we maintain control over our attitudes and actions. An angry person is not someone who is in control—in fact, angry people are probably the most out-of-control people there are. Angry people may feel empowered by their anger—like it is going to give them the authority they will need to fix a situation. But really they have thrust themselves under the authority of whoever it is that has disappointed them.

A person who doesn't get a promotion at work and decides he is going to spend time bad-mouthing the promoted candidate behind his back has really just given the bosses all the confirmation they needed to know that they made the *right* choice. No one wants an out-of-control angry person in leadership within their company. Those bosses aren't going to be thinking, *Gee, I really wish we had hired a lunatic like Paul to be our vice-president of operations.*

Self-control will always help us bring about the results we want inwardly, even if we can do nothing to bring about the results we want to see outwardly. None of us want to be miserable, and misery is a choice. By implementing self-control we will be able to maintain a spirit of peace and joy even when our circumstances claim we should be feeling and acting otherwise.

James Friesen once wrote, "Living from our hearts is not simply doing what our feelings tell us. That would be folly. Living from our hearts means that there is an inner directive that, if governed by the Spirit of God, keeps us on a path that is spiritually attuned to who we are and how God is leading."[3]

Notice that in Galatians 5 it says the *fruit* of the Spirit—not *fruits*—is self-control. Along with self-control, eight other traits are listed: love, joy, peace, patience, kind-

---

[3]James G. Friesen et al., *The Life Model: Living From the Heart Jesus Gave You* (Van Nuys: Shepherd's House, 2000), 6.

ness, gentleness, faithfulness, and goodness. The fruit of the Spirit is not plural. If we are to bear fruit in our lives as Christians, we must learn to grow in all nine areas. Notice anger doesn't appear on that list. But do you see what does? Joy. How in the world can you have joy when your life is spinning out of control? Are we supposed to be happy when our dreams go up in smoke? That's just impossible . . . isn't it?

> You may not be able to change the outcome of your circumstances, but you can always change your attitude.

Hebrews 12:2 tells us that Jesus was able to endure a shameful death on the cross because of the *joy* He knew would be His *afterward.* It also tells us that we can face whatever we are up against and endure. "We do this by keeping our eyes on Jesus, on whom our faith depends from start to finish," it says. Are you catching on yet? Joy is produced in place of anger when we take our eyes off ourselves and place them on Christ. When we stop playing the victim, stop lamenting that life *didn't turn out the way we imagined it,* we are able to embrace joy even in the midst of an arduous journey of which the end result now may no longer be what we always thought it would. You may not be able to change the outcome of your circumstances, but you can always change your attitude. And that's really all we are asked to do.

God does not ask us to fix circumstances we have no control over—other people, nature, unfair decisions made against us—but He does ask us to change our attitudes.

"But when the Holy Spirit controls our lives, He will produce this kind of fruit in us: love, joy, peace, patience, kindness, goodness, faithfulness, gentleness, and self-control" (Galatians 5:22–23a).

Raising the White Flag

One thing that will really help propel us down the road in getting from where we are to where we want to go in life is surrendering the way we think things should happen. We can be almost certain that things won't go according to our detailed plans. Having an attitude of surrender will help us move forward without getting hung up when things don't go our way.

Charles Spurgeon once said, "God is too good to be unkind, too wise to be mistaken, and when you cannot trace His hand, you can always trust His heart." We know this to be true not because of our outward circumstances—those aren't always the best gauges of things. We know it to be true because of what God says to us in His Word:

> *I know what I'm doing. I have it all planned out— plans to take care of you, not to abandon you, plans to give you the future you hope for* (Jeremiah 29:11, The Message).

Ultimately we want the future that we hope for, and many times God wants to give us exactly that. Sometimes, though, He wants to give it to us in a different way and we argue with the process. In an earlier chapter I told you that I felt God leading me out of a life of full-time ministry, and I told you that I eventually found where He wanted me to be—in a sales career. What I held back from mentioning was the plan I entertained in between.

Feeling as if the only thing I was really skilled at was ministry—and teaching God's Word—I felt that was the only way I could provide for a wife. So I decided I would go to seminary and get a master's degree in the hopes that one day I would be able to pastor my own church. The only problem was that I would need a job to support Shannon and me as I went through seminary.

A dad of one of the boys I had discipled in the past was the manager of a local warehouse store and promised that he would bring me on in a management position that would provide enough of an income for Shannon and me to live off of while I went back to school. I would start with the company in our hometown and transfer to the branch in the city and state where the seminary that had accepted me was located. He asked me to give him a month—so I did. Then he asked for another, and then another. . . .

For five months this went on, until one day he called to say his plan of bringing me on board had fallen through due to budget cuts and there was nothing he could do. This happened four months before my wedding, and I had already given my notice at the church where I was working. The pastors at my church felt bad for me, so they offered to move me over to the maintenance department and keep me on staff so I could at least be making some money while I sought God on what to do next.

It was a very humbling time for me, as my job description required me to empty the trash cans of the very same men whom I once taught alongside. *What is going on here,*

Lord? My mind raced with questions. *I thought I heard your voice telling me to leave the staff here at this church. I thought you were showing me that in the coming year I would get to teach your Word in ways I never had before.* Together Shannon and I lamented that things hadn't happened the way we had played them out in our minds.

And one day I realized that working in maintenance was not the answer God had for me. So I called my friend Brian, who is now my district manager, and asked him if he could help me out by bringing me on board with his company. At that time I thought sales was a temporary solution that would still get me to the altar on time. But as my first year in sales—and my first year of marriage—began to unfold, I saw that the heartache I had endured was God's way of giving me the future I hoped for.

In that year alone I was invited to speak more than a handful of times in places as varied as South Dakota, Peru, and Florida—prior to that I had never taught outside of my own church. Shannon and I were offered a contract to write this book. Up until that point I had never written anything longer than a term paper. My career in sales allowed me the flexibility in my schedule that I would need in order to accept these invitations. It provided an income that was more than ample even during times when I would need to take days or weeks off in order to travel and teach God's Word. My thinking had been far too small—I was asking God to give me a small church to teach in *someday.* He wanted to expand my pulpit to include the entire world, and He wanted to give it to me *now.* The future I hoped for came through waving the white flag and surrendering any method I had previously planned on using in getting there.

Sometimes you may feel as if you don't even get to wave the white flag yourself; you feel as if it was waved for you. In moments like these we truly do need to take our eyes off ourselves and place them on the Lord. When we cannot trace His hand, we most certainly need to keep trusting His heart. In *The Message*, Romans 8:5–8 says:

> *Those who think they can do it on their own end up obsessed with measuring their own moral muscle but never get around to exercising it in real life. Those who trust God's action in them find that God's Spirit is in them— living and breathing God! Obsession with self in these matters is a dead end; attention to God leads us out into the open, into a spacious, free life. Focusing on self is the opposite of focusing on God. Anyone completely absorbed in self ignores God, ends up thinking more about self than God. That person ignores who God is and what He is doing. And God isn't pleased at being ignored.*

This passage talks about the tendency of Christians to continue wrestling with sin even when we know we should submit to the ways of the Lord. This can be applied to situations involving anger over God's methods and the pride and arrogance of wanting to do things our way without His help. We are not in control—even when things are going great and we feel like we are in control. At any moment, when things are going according to our own plans, God can flip the switch and cause things to go into a tailspin. We can get off track from our plans in a matter of seconds, but we are never off track according to God's—even when we find ourselves emptying trash cans, wondering what in the world happened to the lives we wanted to live.

It's time we all raised the white flag of surrender and conceded to let God do things His way. His methods are always better suited to us than our own, and they usually produce bigger results than we ever could have imagined. Ephesians 3:20 says: "Now glory be to God! By His mighty power at work within us, He is able to accomplish infinitely more than we would ever dare to ask or hope."

Going With It

As you continue your journey in getting from where you are to where you want to go, you will encounter many varied emotions. Anger, disappointment, and even confusion are just a few. Another one you may experience is jealousy. When it seems like your plans have been thwarted, most certainly it will also seem like everything is coming together a little too perfectly for others. They won't be able to relate to your heartache, and their success will be loudly touted right in front of your face. And in some cases it will appear as if they have run off with your dream.

The best piece of advice I can give you in moments like these is to just go with it. Let go of your own agenda and refuse to have a pity party. Focus your thoughts on other things and take inventory of all you have to be thankful for—and just keep moving forward.

Shannon is not someone who is easily discouraged, but I can always tell when little things begin to build up and really bother her. Sometimes something as simple as going to a local bookstore can open a floodgate in her heart that releases a wave of seemingly overwhelming emotions. On days like these she comes home quiet, not saying much. When my extremely verbal wife runs out of words, I know something is wrong—even when I ask every guy's favorite question, "What's wrong?" and she answers, "Nothing."

When she is ready to talk, she usually says something like this: "I really should stop writing books. [So-and-so] has written almost ten bestsellers, and she got published around the same time I did. Why does God need me if He can just use her?" I usually respond to her by telling her how much I love her and how gifted I believe she truly is, at which point she usually looks at me and says something profound like, "You're biased." Every single time this has ever happened, a few days will pass, and Shannon will receive more than a handful of e-mails from girls and women all over the world—as close to our home as the next city and as far away as Australia, the Netherlands, and the Philippines—telling her what an impact her books have made on their lives. They refer to her as their mentor or their "favorite" author, and slowly she begins to see that it doesn't matter if she doesn't have a whole end cap in the local Barnes & Noble—what matters is that she is changing lives for the glory of Jesus Christ.

In the several years she has been writing, Shannon has learned to just go with it when things don't come together like she wants them to. She has learned to let go of the standard of success she used to measure herself by. She has learned to stop competing with the concept of what she thinks she should be and embrace who she is. And my sweet wife, who likes to be in control of the things in her life, has learned to let go.

If you were angry when you started this chapter, we

hope you have begun the process of finding a feeling that will release you from that anger. If you were out of control, living life on an emotional roller coaster, we hope you are starting to reel yourself back into a place where you can exercise self-control. If you were charging out on the battlefield of life, trying to claim a victory you could never achieve on your own, we hope you are willing to raise your white flag of surrender and let God do things His way. And if you aren't yet where you want to be, we hope that you continue to go with it—and go with God—until you get there.

FOR FURTHER THOUGHT:

1. Describe an instance in the last six months where you felt you lost control of an event and it didn't turn out the way you expected.
2. Is there a person or situation in your life that flares your anger more quickly than anything else? Explain.
3. List three ways you can learn to respond to anger better.
4. Read Romans 11:34–36. Do verses like that give you comfort when confusion sets in and you lose control?
5. What role does jealousy play in your life, and whom are you usually jealous of?

DO IT NOW

Find a feeling. Put this exercise into practice during the next week. When you begin to get aggravated or angry, take a deep breath and identify the real feeling that is hiding somewhere deep inside.

“ *Even if you are on the right track, you will get run* **”**
over if you just sit there.
—Will Rogers

When it comes to getting from where you are to where you want to go in life, you have to start somewhere. Most of the time it doesn't matter where you start exactly; it simply matters that you choose to start at all. We all start from where we are—it's the only choice we have if we want to move toward our goals. The only other option is to stay where we are—but that will not move us forward, and in many cases it will only put us behind in the grand scheme of things.

I (Michael) work for a company that provides excellent stock benefits to those who are with the company a minimum of ten years. After ten years my stock will be fully vested—meaning all of it will be available for me to cash out should I choose to leave the company. I started with my company when I was twenty-one. A lot of guys in my office started in their forties or fifties. At company gatherings I always hear them lamenting that they didn't start with our company back when they were my age. Because I started earlier, I will be able to retire earlier (and with more money in stock).

You cannot go back and start from a place in your life

that you have left behind. And waiting to get to another point in your life before you start working toward your ultimate goal will only put you behind—it robs you of one thing: time.

A man by the name of Robert Fritz once said, "If you limit your choices to only what seems possible or reasonable, you disconnect yourself from what you truly want, and all that is left is a compromise."

A common question we all have when it comes to getting from where we are to where we want to go is, "Where do I start?" And the answer is simply, you start right where you are. No two people will ever start in the exact same place, but we all start somewhere. Do not fall into the trap of believing that you are not at a good spot to start—your starting place is the spot you move *forward* from, not where you end up. You can move forward from anywhere.

So now that we have determined that you can start from right where you are, let's look at three steps you can implement to begin your journey from where you are to where you want to go.

Step #1: Maximize Your Time

There is not enough time in a day. Any of us who have gone to school, worked, and tried to pursue a dream all at the same time know that firsthand. Chances are your schedule is already full—even without your dream and the effort it will take to pursue it. That is why maximizing your time is vital when it comes to pursuing your dream.

For instance, I (Shannon) recently complained to my

friend Annie that I hate getting good ideas for books or chapters when I am in the shower. Since I can't write them down, those ideas tend to literally go down the drain, as I cannot always remember them once I get out. A few weeks later a package arrived containing children's bathtub crayons. *These are so all of your great ideas don't go down the drain,* Annie wrote on a little note tucked inside the package.

So guess what? This chapter was actually outlined on my shower walls before it was ever typed out on this page. I literally opened Annie's package and decided to maximize my time that day by writing out my thoughts as I let conditioner soak into my hair and warm water beat on my back. It was actually really fun, and I am going to try to do it more regularly. As I was scribbling on my walls with these special crayons (if you try this, please do not use regular crayons, as they might not come off), I thought of what a great idea it would be to write some of my life goals on the shower wall, where I would see them every day. Even on days when I don't check my calendar or consult my to-do list, I still shower—so the shower would be an excellent place to stick reminders. It would be a great place to work on committing Scripture to memory too.

Other friends I know listen to books on audio while they drive to and from work. If one of your goals is to grow more spiritually, one of the best things you can do is listen to the Bible on CD while you drive. If you want to advance your career—or even start a new one, for that matter—select a book that will give you great insights into the area where you want to grow, and pop it in as you drive. Sometimes we just don't think about incorporating daily quiet time into our drive.

Think about areas in your life where you have idle time, and look for productive ways to fill that time. By adding just one or two seemingly small things to your day, you could wind up adding years of wisdom and insight to your life. Michael used to read his Bible on his lunch breaks at work—it not only helped him stay in the Word, but it also was a great conversation starter with those who wanted to know about what he believed.

Michael and I also want to share five principles about time that Pastor Kenton Beshore shared with our congregation recently. (If you are interested in hearing the sermon in which he shared these points, ordering information is available in the appendix.)

First he pointed out that *there is a compounding value to investing small amounts of time regularly.* For instance, those of us who exercise regularly know that we can see results by adding several hours of regular exercise to our weekly routines. We don't have to exercise every minute to see these results, but we do need to regularly invest small amounts of time. The same is true when it comes to relationship building or goal reaching. The more frequently we invest small amounts of time into something, the better our results will be.

Secondly, Kenton shared that *neglect has a compounding effect.* Sticking with the exercise analogy, he pointed out that those of us who do not exercise usually reap the consequences of failing to do so. Any of us who have ever been in shape but no longer are know this well. You can have your ideal muscle tone and percentage of body fat, but if you do not maintain it you will lose it. Yesterday, as we tortured our bodies on the reformer equipment at our Pilates studio, my friend Allie said to me between exercises, "How long do we have to keep doing this again?"

"As long as we want to reap the benefits," I said, groaning as I picked up my free weights again. You must invest time and continue to invest time in the areas in which you desire to see a certain result.

Kenton's third point was that *missing any single installment rarely makes a huge impact.* That's why it is so easy for people to get out of shape or get out of fellowship. Missing one day at the gym or one Sunday at church doesn't seem like a big deal at the time, so we tend to slough it off. But if we are not careful, that one installment becomes two and then three, and before we know it we are reaping the consequences of compounded neglect. This is why it is so important to outline your goals and really stick to them.

The fourth point in this particular sermon is that *there is no compounding effect to "urgent" things.* This one was huge for me. At this point Kenton began to bring up a long list of "urgent" things that seem to rob us of our time—reading the newspaper, going online, taking out the trash, piddling around the house. There are things that all of us do when we know we should really be doing other things. And these seemingly urgent things are really time stealers with no compounding effect—they don't count for anything in the long run because they don't build over time when they are added together.

For instance, he used the example of his family. They had dinner together five nights a week for eight years while all four of his boys were living at home. It was a nonnegotiable commitment. There were always "urgent" things popping up at work or with friends that could have kept Kenton's family members from keeping their commitment, but they left those seemingly urgent things undone and ate together as a family. And now that all of his boys are out of the house and his nest is empty, he can look back and say he has no regrets. But if he had tended to all of those urgent things instead, looking back, he wouldn't really be able to account for the time he missed with his family.

"Well, I spent two of those nights having dinner with friends, and three of those nights at the gym. Ten of them were spent counseling others, etc." The list would go on and on, amounting to a bunch of little things that don't compound to have real value. It's like putting your money into a savings account—you put all of your savings in one place so it can compound and grow over time. You don't put five dollars in one account, twenty-five in another, and a hundred in yet another account. That just wouldn't make any sense. Yet so often that is what we do with our time.

> *Invest your time in the people and things that are going to yield you the results you ultimately want.*

Martyred missionary Jim Elliot once said, "Wherever you are, be all there." It is very important that you invest your time in the people and things that are going to yield you the results you ultimately want. Time spent in any other way is time wasted.

Kenton's fifth and final point regarding time was simply that *in critical areas of life, we cannot make up for lost time.* We can always choose to use our time differently and move forward from there, but we cannot make up for the time we wasted or spent in a different way. For twenty-somethings, time is our biggest asset because it does compound. Even long-range goals are within reach as long as we make the investment to take active steps toward getting there each and every day. Don't let another day go by without deciding to take deliberate action in your life. Live intentionally. Make every minute count, and do only what is important and necessary. Everything else robs you of your time.

Step #2: Establish and Grow Key Relationships

Our friend Kathy always says, "Life is all about who you know—that's how you get into heaven, anyway!" In many cases life really is all about who you know. People are often the best tools when it comes to helping us get from where we are to where we want to go. Don't misunderstand what we are saying here. We are in no way condoning *using* other people for your own gain. We're not talking about networking in order to advance yourself. We are, however, talking about building relationships with people who know something about what it is you want to do. Mentors are invaluable. Most successful people have had a mentor who championed their cause somewhere along the way.

I (Shannon) have had a few such women along my path in the writing world. I grew up reading every word written by bestselling author Robin Jones Gunn. Her fictional character Christy Miller came to life in such a way that I felt as if she were a real person. Robin's writings were extremely influential in my preteen and teen years. So when I found out that Robin had agreed to write the foreword for my first book, I was ecstatic. When she invited me to breakfast, and later into a friendship, I thought I was going to faint. She was someone I looked up to in many ways, and whenever we talked, I hung on her every word.

In many ways Robin is responsible for the shaping of my career. She introduced me to some of the coordinators of youth events that I now frequently speak at, and she introduced me to my agent, Janet, who is responsible for connecting me with both of the publishers I am currently writing for. Janet is someone who sees a vision for my career that I can only dream of, and she has enough experience in the industry to help me map out a realistic approach for what I should do next. I know I can put my career in her hands and trust her completely.

Both Robin and Janet have sought to encourage me, uplift me, and push me forward. Without them I would have quit writing long ago. The truth they have spoken into my life and the vision they have cast in me are invaluable. I became wise before my time because of the wisdom these women poured into me. Without them there is no way I could have found myself contracted for ten books in four years.

Everyone needs someone to champion their causes. We all need cheerleaders as well as people who will tell us the honest truth—even when it may hurt our egos but help us meet our goals. Having a personal teacher who is willing to tutor us through whatever it is we want to do—grow spiritually, advance our careers, break into the industry of our dreams—will get us there a lot quicker. Often it is their experience that reminds us that we all start at the beginning and move up, even when there are days we feel like quitting—but we should never give in.

Finding a mentor can be tough. I was always the type of person who desperately wanted a spiritual mentor. Wanting to grow in my walk with the Lord, I felt as if I needed to learn from someone who had been there before. And out of the two women I ever got enough courage to ask, one had to say no because she was leaving for the mission field, and the other politely declined and later admitted it was because she was having an affair. (I was thankful she didn't say yes—otherwise I could have ended up very messed up by having someone like that disciple me.)

When it comes to Robin and Janet, Robin sort of found me through my writing, and through Robin I found Janet. There really isn't a formula for finding a mentor. You just have to pray that God will direct your paths and place the right people alongside of you at the right time. Many times the relationships that have the most profound impact on us aren't those with formal titles. If you asked Robin and Janet if they were my mentors, I'm sure they would hesitate to strap on such a weighty title. But I have moved them to that position of respect in my life and have allowed them to speak truth to me in ways I don't let just anyone speak truth to me.

If you are in a place where you really want to get from where you are to where you want to go, seek out someone (or many someones) who can help you get there. Ask around; the people you know may be able to introduce you to someone they know who fits the description of what you are looking for in a mentor and friend (after all, it was Robin who introduced me to Janet).

Step #3: Don't Wait for All of the Pieces to Fit

Most of us have grown so accustomed to heating things up in the microwave or eating fast food that we have come to expect a quick fix for everything. We don't understand why everything can't just come together for us at once. When all of the pieces don't instantly fit for us, we give up on our goals—or at least on our current method of reaching them.

A perfect example of this is single twentysomethings who want to get involved in their church but feel as if they can't because they aren't married and don't have kids. Trust us, we both totally understand. We were single not that long ago. We volunteered with a high school youth group where the youth pastor always talked about how he wanted more young married couples to volunteer because they had homes they could invite the high school students to. The stigma of being a single in ministry has plagued us too.

But it is not a reason to avoid getting involved. The truth is, single people usually have more time than married people to commit to things outside of the home—and they definitely have more time than married people with kids. For every relationship you add to your life, the more of your free time you will need to devote to making that relationship work. Relationships just take time.

Do not wait for all of the pieces to fit perfectly. Chances are they might *never* fit perfectly. About eight months before writing this chapter, we moved to a new town and began searching for a new church. Once we found the church that we now call our home, we decided that we wanted to get plugged in right away so that we could meet new people and begin building relationships with the new community God had given us.

Our church heavily promotes small groups because of how easy it is to build honest and deep relationships in that sort of environment. At a church with ten thousand members, it could be easy to otherwise get lost. So we joined a small group for our life stage—young married couples. It was awkward to join a group with two other couples who already knew each other. Sure, we thought about waiting until we had attended our church longer before getting involved. But we knew if we didn't join a small group right away, we would run the risk of never joining one. So awkwardness and all, we joined—and we loved it.

We cannot wait for all of the pieces to fit. If you want to get involved in ministry, get involved. If you want to join a small group, join one. But if you try to make something work that just isn't working, maybe you are trying the wrong thing—maybe you're in the wrong ministry or in a small group with the wrong people. Maybe you are in the wrong career or working for the wrong company. Perhaps you are majoring in the wrong subject. It is okay to change your mind along the way. If you set a goal for yourself and lose your passion along the way, then set a new goal for yourself and start—from right where you are— working toward that goal instead. There is no rule that says trying something means you have to stick with it forever.

> *It is okay to change your mind along the way. . . . There is no rule that says trying something means you have to stick with it forever.*

Sometimes the hardest part about knowing where to start is that we really *do* know where to start—we just wish we could take an easier path or start from somewhere farther down the road. But we can't. We are where we are, and we aren't going to get anywhere else unless we deliberately choose to move forward. So what's it going to be? Are you going to keep standing there wondering where to start? Or are you going to actually do something about your goal and start working toward it *now*?

FOR FURTHER THOUGHT:

1. Have you started pursuing your goals and dreams, or are you still on the starting line? If you're on your way, what motivated you to start? If you are still stuck, what will it take to motivate you to get going?

2. How can you better maximize the time in your weekly schedule?

3. Have you ever had a mentor? If so, describe your relationship. If not, how could having a mentor help you at this stage in your life?

4. Describe a time in the past where God called you to do something—or go somewhere—and all of the pieces didn't fit yet.

5. What is the number one thing that holds you back from getting started on pursuing your dreams?

DO IT NOW

Discover five reasons why *now* is the perfect time to start pursuing your goals and dreams. Write them down and review them regularly. Don't wait another moment—do it right now!

66 *Economy is half the battle of life; it is not so hard* **99**
    to earn money as to spend it well.
    —*C. H. Spurgeon*

It doesn't matter how much money you have, because you never seem to have enough. There is always the perpetual desire, sometimes disguised as a "need," for more. When it comes to living out your dreams and achieving your goals, you will need money. It is almost always part of the equation when it comes to getting from where we are to where we want to go.

Through the writing of this book, we have encountered countless young people whose dreams have been put on hold due to financial constraints. One woman—whom we told you about earlier—cannot venture onto the mission field due to the amount of debt she has. A particular young couple cannot adopt because they are financially strapped, and the thousands of dollars adoptions take is just too far out of their reach. With every story we heard, our hearts broke. It doesn't need to be like this. No matter how small our incomes are, they can be the very fuel we need to fund the pathway to our dreams. Early in our marriage we were taught some invaluable lessons about money—those same lessons will make up the bulk of this chapter.

Since we are simply your peers—and not financial experts—we will mention a few outside resources we have found helpful at the end of this chapter. And we will post a more exhaustive list, and some interactive tools, at our Web site *www.yourmomentisnow.com.*

We used to think finances were only a problem for the cash-strapped and debt-laden until several conversations with other twenty- and thirtysomethings changed our perspective. Even the wealthy tend to find themselves coming up short at times because everyone tends to adjust their lifestyles to their incomes—and sometimes they even attempt to stretch their lifestyles well past what their incomes can afford.

One night Shannon and I (Michael) sat around drinking coffee with friends—all in their twenties or thirties—from various income brackets. Several drove luxury vehicles in spectacular shape. One couple was making payments on a home worth upward of nine hundred thousand dollars (yeah, welcome to life in Southern California). After a while the conversation made a natural progression from careers to finances.

"I'm particularly concerned about the change in lifestyle I will have to endure in order to start a family," one guy said. He made it clear that his current lifestyle was fully dependent on both his and his wife's incomes and that there wasn't a lot left over after all was said and done each month.

Another young man, who is self-employed with a commission-based income (like me), shared that he was concerned about how much longer he and his wife could continue living off of her steady income while work waxed and waned for him. These conversations amazed us because both of these couples made decent six-figure incomes. And still, at the end of the day, there wasn't enough to go around.

Wouldn't that be nice, you might be thinking at the mention of such a sizable wad of cash. But the heart of finances for young people isn't what you make—it's what you *spend.* After delving deep into this subject and consulting everyone from our peers to the cofounder of the largest financial ministry in the world (more on that later), we found that the financial problems most of us face boil down to one thing: what we owe versus what we own.

> *The heart of finances for young people isn't what you make—it's what you spend.*

The Great Masquerade

Finances, for most people, are about keeping up with appearances. I (Shannon) will never forget a conversation I had with a friend who was trying to talk me into purchasing a home that was several hundred thousand dollars more than Michael and I could afford.

As I carefully explained why Michael and I weren't willing to use creative financing to get into a home that would cost more than we could *really* afford (as opposed to what we could *appear* to afford while strapping ourselves to where we almost couldn't move), this friend finally cut into my explanation rather sharply.

"Well, I guess only *some* of us are willing to take risks," she spat. When it came to cash on hand, my friend and I were very different. I saved as much as possible, and she spent it so fast that she couldn't even keep track of it. But to the naked eye, because of all of her nice things, my friend appeared to be several income levels ahead of me. In all honesty, the biggest difference between us was debt—she had tons, and I had none.

Other young people we've met have tried to make cutbacks in their spending—they no longer give out gifts at weddings, birthday parties, or holidays, but they continue to keep up on the latest trends in their own clothing and music choices.

Managing your finances well is a lot like dieting—crash dieting doesn't work long-term, but a complete lifestyle change will help you keep unwanted pounds off. The same is true for your spending habits. Choosing to skip out on buying your friend a birthday gift or withholding your ten percent from the tithe box isn't going to help if you are still shelling out the big bucks for your coffee addiction at Starbucks. We have met far too many people who try to make cuts in the wrong places rather than sitting down and figuring out the best way to spend their money.

For most of us, the concept of a budget isn't too appealing. We may claim we don't need one—that was always my excuse. Others use budgeting software to keep track of spending—*after* the fact. If we spend more than we have, the numbers on our screen simply go red, and so do the numbers in our bank account. This isn't helpful—nor is choosing to ignore the fact that the checkbook needs to be balanced, and a check bounces as a result. Credit cards aren't much help either, as they trick us into thinking we can afford things we really can't. They become a tool that helps us keep up appearances while racking up debt.

Recently we visited a friend who was house-sitting for his wealthy aunt and uncle at their beach house. Just for fun he decided to take us out for a spin in their brand-new Mercedes convertible.

"My uncle sure knows how to do things right," he yelled as the salty air whipped through our hair. "He never buys a car. He always leases them. So when he gets sick of one, he just trades it in for something else. Before this he had a Jaguar."

What our friend failed to realize was that in leasing all of these vehicles, his uncle was constantly making car payments—and probably hefty ones at that. By choosing not to purchase a car, he never wound up owning one. He never drove anything that was paid off. As two people who are currently driving paid-off vehicles, Michael and I can attest to the fact that not having a car payment can free up tons of cash for other things—like starting your own business, joining a gym, saving for a house, or going back to school. But if you were to ask the average person on the street if they would rather drive a leased Mercedes or a paid-off Honda, our guess is that most would opt for the Mercedes. Why? Because we would rather *look* wealthy than *be* wealthy. Have you ever noticed that the people we consider to be the wealthiest are those with the most stuff and not the most cash? That really is a backward mentality.

What most people don't understand is that having something in your possession doesn't mean you actually own it. Seriously, stop and take a personal inventory for a moment and add up everything you have that is financed—a TV, a car, a pair of shoes on your credit card, maybe even your college education. If you are still making payments on it, you don't own it and it isn't really yours. It *appears* to be yours, and perhaps that gives you a sense of security that is worth the interest you are paying on that item. But chances are that "security" will wear off long before the payments stop.

Now that you are probably genuinely depressed, let's look at four ways we can make the most of what we have and use our bank accounts as a tool in getting us from where we are to where we want to go.

Step #1: Setting Up a Spending Plan

Recently Michael and I met a young couple who both had decent, although modest, incomes. They *appeared* to live comfortably (are you noticing a trend with this word yet?): New clothes, expensive shoes, and fun dates defined their lifestyle. But with no savings and a little overspending, they found themselves in quite a bind one month when it came time to pay their mortgage. With no other choice, they were forced to humble themselves and seek financial assistance. Although my heart breaks for them, I cannot help but wonder if that assistance came a little too easily. Only time will tell if they learned from their mistake. Although Michael and my circumstances were never that dire and we have always had at least some savings, we see how easy it can be to out-spend yourself. A man who works with Michael's company told him that he had initially retired years earlier—but he spent all of his retirement money and had to return to work so he could make more.

That is why having a spending plan is so important. Whether you are single or married, in college or working in the career of your dreams, establishing good financial habits now—in your twenties—will help you tremendously throughout the rest of your life as long as you continue to apply them. Did you know that the average American family spends ten percent more than they make no matter what their salary is?[1]

For us, the starting place on our road to financial freedom was developing a spending plan. We sat down and tallied up all of our monthly expenses (we kept receipts for an entire month to help us calculate variable things like grocery, gas, entertainment, etc.). All of our costs were divided up into very specific categories (rent, phone bill, eating out, etc.), and then we subtracted our monthly expenses from our monthly income—when the number came up negative, we began to evaluate the areas in which we were overspending. Who knew we consumed that much Chinese food from the place around the corner?

At that point we created a spreadsheet and wrote the amount of each monthly bill beneath the heading for each category. For variable expenses we came up with a number we both agreed was reasonable—and within our reach. The key to setting a spending plan that works is found in *not* creating a budget that doesn't allow for enjoyable expenditures—going on a date, getting your hair done, buying a new CD, etc. If you cut out all fun or excess

---

[1]Steven B. Smith, *Money for Life* (Chicago: Dearborn, 2004), 35.

spending, you will quickly become frustrated and throw out your spending plan altogether. Make room for going out to eat or going on vacation, but put your priorities in order.

We found that the traditional "envelope system" that most of our grandparents and great-grandparents used works great. During the Great Depression era, many people made an actual envelope for each of their expenses and put a set amount of cash in each one. When the envelope was empty, they stopped spending because there was nothing left to spend. Of course, we are an almost cashless society today, so using cash for everything might not work for you. But the principle still keeps you from overspending.

You can create a spreadsheet on your computer and place a different spending category in every box across the top or side of your grid. Then each time you get paid, divide your paycheck and allot it to the categories that need funding. Every time you make a purchase, make sure you deduct the money from each "envelope." Consult your spreadsheet before going shopping and never spend more than what you have in each envelope.

This will help you stay (and even get) out of debt. If you are in debt, make an envelope for each of your debts and try to pay more than the minimum each month—this will help you pay off your debts more quickly. As you pay off one debt, use the "snowball" approach and take the money you were paying toward that debt and add it to another debt to help accelerate paying it off too.

If you are not good at math (that would be me) but this concept of the envelope system appeals to you, you might want to check out an online system that automatically establishes and funds "envelopes" with the information you provide. It is a tried-and-true system (we have used it and it is amazing), and it is offered through Crown Financial Ministries, which is one of the most reputable financial ministries out there. For more information visit *www.crown.mvelopes.com.*

Once you begin keeping track of your money, it will be easier to see where you might be overspending—which ultimately could be why you are unable to come up with the funds you need to get where you want to go. You might have to alter your lifestyle a bit in order to avoid overspending—we don't have cable television because we want to be able to put more money in savings each month. During baseball season this is hard for us, but we still think it is worth it. To compensate for our lack of cable, we make sure we keep our "date night" envelope full enough to catch a game on television at ESPN Zone or at a local pizza place.

If you find that you are doing everything in your power to set a realistic spending plan and you live by it, yet you are still coming up short each month, you might not only be overspending—you might also be under-earning. In that case, you will need to seriously evaluate your earning potential in your current job and consider taking on a second job or find a new job entirely. We recently met a twenty-one-year-old woman who wanted to purchase a car and avoid having to make payments. She found a used car that would suit her needs perfectly, and she took a side job on weekends to save specifically for her car. Her other job provides for all of the other categories mapped out on her spending plan, but she knew in order to buy a car she would need to generate more income.

If you are like Michael and me, sometimes it is hard to know whether an expense is worth it. So try asking yourself a few questions: Is this necessary? Can I do it for less somewhere else? Is this impulsive or planned? Am I being persuaded to purchase this item?[2] Trust us, questions like that really take the emotion out of shopping. They allow you to think clearly and weigh your current spending decisions against your future goals. We asked ourselves these questions when we were furnishing our first apartment. Knowing we would keep this furniture only until we moved into a house, we were able to find some great deals. Our furniture looked great and did the job, even if it wasn't our first choice.

Step #2: Set Short- and Long-Term Financial Goals

About one month into our marriage, we were introduced to a resource put out by Crown Financial Ministries called the Crown Money Map. Essentially it is a roadmap for financial planning, with Scripture verses backing up each "destination" on the map. You start at destination one—which involves saving one thousand dollars for emergencies and establishing a spending plan. You end on destination seven—with your retirement completely funded and all of the time in the world to volunteer to do the Lord's work—or in other words, to live out the dream He put in your heart without money being an obstacle.

---

[2]Richard Paul Evans, *Five Lessons a Millionaire Taught Me* (New York: Fireside, 2004), 55–63.

You can view the map online for free at *www.crown.org/moneymap*.

Whether the map is helpful to you or not, it is highly important that you set both short- and long-term financial goals for yourself. The short-term goals are vital to make sure you stick with your plan long enough to reach your long-term ones. Mark Twain once said, "The secret of getting ahead is getting started. The secret of getting started is breaking your complex, overwhelming tasks into small manageable tasks, and then starting on the first one."

Let's say your long-term goal is to start your own business. Short-term goals for that goal could be saving a certain amount of money by a certain amount of time and/or setting aside a specific amount from each of your current paychecks. With every dime you put in savings, you will be ten cents closer to living your dream. Don't get discouraged if you have to start out small—notice the Crown Money Map begins by asking you to save a mere one thousand dollars and ends with you having your entire retirement funded and your home completely paid off. You have to start small in order to make it all the way to the end. One thing we have learned as we have been saving for our own goals is that saving gets easier as time goes on and you see the amount in your savings account grow. There is something gratifying about seeing a number with a lot of zeros behind it on your monthly bank statement.

Step #3: Keep a Little Bit of Everything You Earn

Have you ever noticed that many times the most important things seem to be the hardest to do? It's not that they are hard in and of themselves. They are just always so easy to put off. Saving a portion out of every paycheck falls into this category. Thankfully Shannon and I (Michael) have been able to work out our spending plan so that we can live exclusively off my income and put all of Shannon's income into savings. This has catapulted us across several destinations on the Money Map and is allowing us to get close to a few of our larger goals. Not everyone is in a position where they can save one whole income, but everyone should attempt to find a way to save at least something at the end of every month.

Earlier we admitted we don't have cable because we'd rather save. A similar cutback may become necessary for you if you want to save as well. But if you have a dream that needs funding, there is no better way to go about it than to save. Investing can be good too, but you should at least have some savings. Most financial experts suggest having at least three to eight months of living expenses in case of emergencies. We know one twentysomething who

quickly lost ten thousand dollars because he opted to invest with friends rather than save. We have another friend who decided to sock money away around the same time this guy chose to invest. The first guy wound up out ten thousand dollars while the other guy found himself with forty thousand dollars in hand.

It's no secret that most savings accounts won't yield a lot of interest, but there are other secure options when it comes to saving. Try opening a money market account, which can earn you around four percent on the money you invest. A Certificate of Deposit (CD) is a good option if you don't mind not being able to draw your money out of the bank for six months to two years. You can learn more about these types of accounts and find competitive rates at *www.bankrate.com.*

If you have a dream that requires money to make it happen, chances are you will only get there by saving. So discipline yourself now and start saving a little bit of everything you make. Little bits can add up to large sums rather quickly if you are disciplined. The Bible even talks about this principle in Matthew 25:14–30, known commonly as the parable of the talents. A man went on a trip and entrusted each of his three servants with some of his money. The first two turned a profit, and the third man buried it so he wouldn't lose what he already had. In verse 27 his boss responds to him by saying, "Well, you should at least have put my money into the bank so I could have some interest." And with that, he took the money away from his servant. Save—earn interest and earn a profit off of what you already have.

Step #4: Tithe Faithfully and Give Generously

Ultimately everything we have belongs to God—it is from Him, and He has given it to us for our use. We know that can be hard to fathom sometimes when it seems like we work so hard for our paychecks. But it is true nonetheless—Psalm 50:10–12 gives an exhaustive list of some of the things God owns. Suffice to say, He really does own it all. We have met a lot of young people who don't tithe at all or don't tithe "as much as they should." Not too long ago we were both in that boat as well. Sometimes it can be so hard to write that tithe check when there doesn't even seem like there is enough money to pay the bills. But recently I (Shannon) chatted on the phone with Howard

Dayton, cofounder of Crown Financial Ministries. Since Michael and I use so many of Crown's resources in our own life, I thought I would see if Mr. Dayton was available to share some insights with me for this chapter in the book. Graciously he made time for me on his busy calendar.

> God has a long track record of financially blessing those who do not withhold their resources from Him.

One of the things he stressed most to me in the half hour we talked was the importance of tithing and giving. He said that many times He thinks God's attitude toward us is, "If you are faithful to me, you will see that I am faithful to you." Now, Mr. Dayton wasn't saying that we can earn God's blessings, but he was referring to the fact that God has a long track record of financially blessing those who do not withhold their resources from Him.

Michael and I have consistently seen the Lord bless us with extra income or gift cards to some of our favorite restaurants and stores when we take a risk and write a tithe check even when it doesn't make financial sense. We live off of Michael's commission-based income. Even my income—which we also tithe from—is variable. So some months are definitely tighter for us than other months. But many times it is in taking a risk that a blessing is received.

Recently we agreed to go on a missions trip to another country for two and a half weeks. Not only did we need to raise support for the trip, but we needed to set aside money to pay our bills while we were gone. Being self-employed or commission-based, we don't get vacation time or paid sick days. At first no support came in. We were forced to make our first payment toward the trip ourselves—but we were confident God wanted us to go, so we did it. Then slowly a few checks trickled in. Not too long before our deadline, two separate people (one whom we didn't even send a support letter to) came to us with checks made out to us instead of the missions agency.

"If this is more than the balance you owe on the trip, put it toward your bills for the month," they told us. "We want to be part of your trip in any way we can." God's graciousness toward us through the generosity of these people left us amazed. We were too stunned for words. It took us a few minutes before we could even form the words to say thank you. We hadn't really shared that side of our need with anybody.

That is how God works. When we risk it all and give Him the small portion He specifically asks for, He gives us back one-hundredfold. On top of giving to the Lord and His work, it is also important to make yourself available to be used by Him to meet the needs of His people.

For us, we decided that in addition to tithing to our church, we wanted to support twelve additional ministries in 2006—one for each month of the year. We chose six within the United States and six outside of the United States. They ranged from missionary families we knew personally and wanted to support, to nonprofit Christian organizations that depend on donations to keep functioning. Some months we felt things get tight right around the time the check was due, but we gave anyway. Other months our increase was so abundant that it wasn't hard to cut the check. But either way, there was always money to give.

In the process of giving, the strangest thing happened. Michael and I discovered that a sense of gratitude deeper than any we had experienced before began to fill our hearts. Gratitude began to weed out any sense of greed that could have easily taken root in our hearts and in our lives. We began to look forward to writing our donation checks each month. It became like a game for us—we looked for ways to add more and more to the amount we were able to give each month. I can honestly say that I have never been so excited to give away thousands of dollars. When we were preparing for our missions trip, we experienced what it is like to be on the receiving end of such a blessing, and that made being on the giving end even more rewarding. Being God's financial tool to meet someone else's genuine need is perhaps one of the greatest privileges a person can ever experience. We challenge you to take the risk and try it sometime. Give.

Financial Freedom = Spiritual Freedom

Larry Burkett, the late cofounder of Crown Financial Ministries, used to say, "You cannot be financially bound and be spiritually free."[3] And that is very true. Debt and unwise spending can truly prevent you from achieving all God dreams to give you in life. Obedience is a huge factor in whether we receive rewards—not salvation but rewards. Money is an area where we could all probably afford to be

---

[3]Larry Burkett, *Debt-Free Living* (Chicago: Moody, 1989), 57–58.

a little wiser and a lot more obedient to Christ and His commands.

If money is an obstacle for you today, take a good long look at why it is an obstacle—and then take the steps you need to implement change. Financial freedom is only a few steps away.

FOR FURTHER THOUGHT:

1. Have you ever felt constricted by a budget? After reading about having a "spending plan," how have your views on budgets changed?

2. Who puts the most pressure on you to spend money? Who encourages you the most to save?

3. Do you tend to be an impulsive buyer, or do you do your homework and research where you will be able to find the best deal?

4. What financial goals do you currently have? How do you plan on reaching them?

5. Do you currently save each month? How can you increase your savings?

DO IT NOW

Establish a spending plan. Reread step #1 and move forward from there. Work on it until it begins to click for you. It takes roughly three months for a budget to begin working correctly—adjusting your first draft is a normal part of the process. Stick with it—you'll love the end result.

" *People often say that motivation doesn't last.* **"**
Well, neither does bathing—that's why we
recommend it daily.
—Zig Ziglar

It seems like I (Shannon) wasn't in my twenties very long before I began setting more goals than I could possibly keep up with. Financially I wanted to get to a certain place, physically I wanted to achieve specific things, and professionally I wanted to grow and expand in many different ways.

Whether I achieved my goals always depended on one thing: how motivated I was to keep moving forward when getting to my goal was no longer easy and the thrill of finally having a plan had worn off. It is one thing to figure out what you need to do (or want to do), and it is an entirely separate thing to actually do it—or keep doing it. You can usually tell how important something is to someone based on their motivation to follow through with it.

Our friend Chris races mountain bikes. Obviously, like most people who race, he wants to win. To him, riding mountain bikes is not just a hobby, it's a way of life. There are stretches of time where almost all of his weekends are filled with races. When he goes home from church on

Sunday afternoons, he doesn't sit in front of the television to relax—he goes out and rides. His commitment to being able to perform well in races is seen in his daily diet—high proteins and low fats for him. Chris's motivation to win a race on the weekend causes him to make certain choices (both big and small) in other areas of life throughout the week.

Now, granted, achieving a short-term goal like winning a race on the weekend can be a lot simpler than achieving a goal you have held on to and pursued for years. Some goals take more time than others to be achieved. The higher you set your goal, the longer it will probably take to get there. For instance, Michael and I really want to buy a house, and our goal isn't just to *get into* a house we can't really afford thanks to creative financing. Our goal is to be well on our way to owning a home free and clear. We have made the commitment not to buy until we can put twenty percent down. To give you a little perspective, we live in an area where two-bedroom *condos* can sell for upwards of eight hundred thousand dollars. Although something in that price range is not our target, you can see we live in a market where it might take us a significant amount of time before achieving our goal.

Now, we have taken several active steps toward reaching our goal. As we mentioned in the last chapter, we live on one income and save the other, and we use a spending plan. We also save any extra income (like bonuses) that we can. But recently we noticed that our motivation was waning. Diligently making sacrifices gets old when you feel like you are not getting close enough to your goal. We figured within two to three years we should be in a position where we could entertain the idea of becoming home-owners. One year into our savings pattern, we found that we were right on track. But *being* on track and *feeling* on track are two entirely different things when your goal is still a long way off.

I decided we needed something to keep us (especially me) motivated. So when a flyer came in the mail advertising a new housing development in the area where we want to live and in the price range we were saving to afford, I concocted a plan. When Michael called from work later that day, I asked him if he was willing to go with me to tour the models. I prefaced my question with the fact that I knew we weren't ready to buy yet, but I was still unsure of how he would react. To my delight, he understood why I was asking right away.

"I think it's a great idea," he said enthusiastically. "This way we can have a picture of what we are saving for in our heads each time we put more money away. When do you want to go?" Without even looking for it, Michael and I had stumbled upon one of the greatest secrets to remaining motivated while working toward a long-term goal.

The Power of Dreaming

When Michael and I went to tour the models, we weren't looking to buy, but we were looking to dream. The key to continuing to stay motivated when your goal is still a long way off is to continue to dream. The moment you stop dreaming is the moment you will fail to remain motivated. After all, you have to remember why you are making sacrifices in the first place. If you are slaving away at a part- or full-time job while continuing to go to school, and you feel like your social life is nonexistent, you are in a tough spot. For you, this could be the do-or-die moment. But if you think about how much you will enjoy your work when you are finally doing what you love, or if you think of the extra income your career of choice could provide you once you get your degree, those things can motivate you to keep going when you would otherwise give up.

Aristotle once said, "The soul never thinks without a picture." So one of the surest ways for you to actually stay motivated to get from where you are to where you want to go is to paint yourself a very vivid mental picture of what you want your life to be like on the other side. Having this picture will not only help you keep going, but it will also help you measure whether the steps you are taking are going to get you to the specific place you want to go. For instance, Michael and I have Disneyland passes, as do some of our friends and family members. If we were to tell friends of ours to meet us at Disneyland but never gave any clearer directives than that, chances are even if we all made it to Disneyland, we would probably not meet up with one another. If we said, "Meet us in front of the Pizza Port in Tomorrowland at five o'clock," there is a much better chance that we will all make it there at the right time.

Our friend Allie was attending a local cosmetology school with the intentions of becoming a hairdresser. A few months into her program she began to realize that because of a recent low rating her school received from the state board, her chances of getting a job at a competitive top-notch salon would be hindered due to poor training.

So she withdrew from this school and put herself on the waiting list to be enrolled in a better program at a different school the following term, and she began inquiring about the possibility of an apprenticeship in the meantime. Sure, it was a seemingly slower route since she took a semester off. But it was going to help get her to her specific destination—a top-notch salon—a lot more quickly. She had a picture in her mind of the type of salon that she wanted to work in, and she looked for the best way to go about making that picture into a reality.

Earlier in the book we talked about the importance of using pictures when setting your goals (remember the photo of Hawaii tucked next to your ATM card?). Having a picture—either mental or physical—to hold on to becomes vital at this stage in working toward your goal.

I vividly remember a time growing up where the mom of one of my closest friends was dieting. She taped a magazine photo of a slim model to the refrigerator door. And you know what? She was less tempted to reach for the ice cream after dinner. Somewhere along the line we have lost the freedom to dream. Chances are there has been a critic somewhere who told us that we just simply can't make it all the way to our goal. Do you know how many people have told Michael and me that we will never reach our goal of being able to put twenty percent down on a home in the area we want to move to? Almost all of those people used creative financing to get into a home they couldn't afford, and many were eventually forced to sell, sometimes at a loss. Their lack of motivation to set and stick to a goal like ours caused them to try to derail us. No one wants to watch someone else accomplish what they believe they cannot. It is so much easier to believe that something cannot be accomplished than it is to stay motivated and disciplined and actually do it.

Dieting and exercise are good examples. I have never been a super athletic person. For the first couple decades of my life it seemed as if I was blessed with a good metabolism. But like I mentioned earlier, something changed when I turned twenty. Suddenly I had to work harder at keeping pounds off. Many girls I know chose to let the pounds pile up, and for a short time I did too. I bought into the excuse that I just wasn't born lucky enough to be thin, and I would have to settle for something a little heavier, called "average."

It wasn't until I started watching what I ate and exercising three times a week that I began to understand that a higher level of fitness and a smaller pant size could be achieved. Shortly after I started losing weight and toning up, a friend of mine (who has gained a significant amount of weight over the years) looked at me with disgust as others began to comment on how well my routine was working. Somewhere along the way she had lost sight of the reality that her dream of being thin could be attained if she was willing to stay motivated and work for it.

The concept of having a picture in your mind as you work toward your goals goes all the way back to the Old Testament. In Genesis 13:14–17 the Lord appears to Abraham (who at that point was still known as Abram) and says, "Look as far as you can see in every direction. I am going to give all this land to you and your offspring as a permanent possession. And I am going to give you so many descendants that, like dust, they cannot be counted!

Take a walk in every direction and explore the new possessions I am giving you."

Talk about having a clear picture in your mind of where it is you are going. I don't think the Lord could have made it any clearer than that. But there was one problem—Abram didn't have any descendants and he was getting older. With a wife who was barren, all he had to hold on to was a picture and a promise from God. It was many years later when that picture began to take the shape of reality for Abram. It is my earnest belief that God gave him that picture so he would stay motivated and wouldn't lose heart.

Years later, in Genesis 37, Abraham's great-grandson Joseph began having a series of God-given dreams. On more than one occasion he dreamed that his brothers would one day bow down to him. For the eleventh son out of twelve, the concept was ridiculous. Even his father, who favored Joseph, grew angry with him when he shared his dream. The dream was even part of what prompted his ten older brothers to sell him into slavery. Thirteen years, one long prison sentence, and one life-threatening famine later, Joseph's dream came true when he was number two to Pharaoh in Egypt and his brothers came to Egypt begging for food. I'm almost positive the dream crossed his mind more than once during his prison stint, especially since God had given Joseph the divine gift of interpreting dreams.

Both Abraham and Joseph were given pictures to hold on to as a way of staying motivated for the long gap of time between receiving the pictures and receiving what those pictures represented. The reason for this is probably the same reason God occasionally takes His sweet time before letting us realize our dreams as well: We must *become ready* to receive the picture and fulfill the dream.

The Process of Becoming

Most of us have read, or at least heard of, Margery Williams' classic children's book *The Velveteen Rabbit*. In the book there is a particularly moving scene where the rabbit (a child's toy) asks the old gray horse (also a child's toy) how you become one of the boy's favorite and most loved animals. And his answer was, "It doesn't happen all at once. . . . You become. It takes a long time."

It's the same with us. We are constantly in the process of becoming. We have no control over that. We do, however, control who it is we become. Many times we must be made ready for what lies ahead before we can receive it. Sure, we can start with a picture of what it is we want and what it is we believe God wants for us. But just because we hold a picture in our mind doesn't mean we are ready for it.

Before I (Michael) married—or even met—Shannon, I held a picture of what I wanted the woman I married to be like. One bad experience was all it took for me to make some very specific adjustments to my list of what I was looking for. But I had refined that list long before I was ready for Shannon to come walking into my life. Sure, I used to ask (and sometimes even beg) God to bring the woman He had for me quickly, but for a time that prayer went unanswered.

Actually, He did answer that prayer. I just didn't like the answer I was getting. Not many of us like to be told "not yet." At first that answer can seem even worse than a no. At least with a no you can give up hope, grieve the death of a dream, and move on to something else. With a "not yet," you are forced to wait. And you will wait in vain if you do not actively work on the art of becoming.

Becoming what? you may ask. Becoming who you want to be, who God wants you to be, and who you need to be before some of these huge pieces can start coming together in your life. I am not talking about outward things here. I am talking about matters of the heart. This sense of becoming is an inward process—one that is centered on your growth in Christ and your character. It is not about who you appear to be but about who you *really* are. When it comes down to it, most of us will admit that there have been moments during our twenties where we looked in the mirror and wondered who we were.

Sure, we all want to feel grown-up and like we have it all together. But deep down there are many moments when we don't feel like we have any of that. We don't know who we are. We have only a vague idea of where we want to go, but most of the time we don't have the slightest idea of how to get there. Moments like this are excellent starting places for the process of becoming. You can't really become anything authentic when you are pretending you are something you are not, so these brief windows of vulnerability are good for our souls.

Many times it is in the moments we have the least amount of clarity about what we are supposed to do, and what we should do, that we can be the most honest about what it is we really want to do. The process of becoming goes hand in hand with the concept of dreaming. In order to become you have to dream wide. Although I certainly don't have all of the answers, I can offer a few suggestions on how to jump-start the becoming process in your life.

> *The process of becoming goes hand in hand with the concept of dreaming. In order to become you have to dream wide.*

Dreaming on Paper

There are a few approaches you can take to beginning the becoming process. I'll start by telling you the method Shannon would choose, and I will follow with my choice. You can pick whichever method appeals to your personality.

Not too long ago, as she mentioned, Shannon completed a Bible study program that was focused on helping her figure out what it was she wanted to do with her life and how she wanted to spend her time. Many of the exercises that appealed to her freaked me out so much that I couldn't follow through with them. One such exercise was titled "A View From the Porch Swing."

The exercise asks you to imagine yourself sitting on your front porch at the age of seventy-five, eighty-five, or ninety-five and think of all the things you want to make sure you have accomplished by that time. You write down the things that would give you the deepest sense of regret if they went undone. The catch is you are to write your reflection in present tense, as if you really are that old and the things you desperately want to do really have happened. Example statements from the workbook include: *I have stayed in great physical shape, I finished college, I was the top salesman in my company, I repaired a broken relation-ship with _____, I made my spouse feel like my first priority after God, etc.*[1]

For Shannon this activity brought clarity. By doing it she saw how she should be spending her time in order to look back without any regrets. She saw relationships that needed work and the investment of time. She mapped out several things she could work on in her career that would help her finish where she wanted to finish. A long look ahead, and then a reflective look back over the years that are still in her future, helped Shannon understand who it was she wanted to become and who it was God wanted her to become. She took an inventory of her gifts and cir-cumstances and mulled over several Bible verses in the process. Shannon emerged from her hypothetical front porch well on her way to becoming. Her choices from that point on began to reflect who she wanted to become.

I, on the other hand, found the concept of looking that many years into the future downright overwhelming. Thinking about hitting thirty is about as far as my mind can go right now. A process that was more appealing to me was the one Margaret Becker outlines in her book *Coming Up for Air*. I'll let Margaret explain the process to you in her own words:

> *What if my life were a fresh page? What if I could write it from this day forward, no holds barred? What if I could make plans and schemes that would actually affect things, knowing that God could interrupt my plans at any given moment if I were off track, or if He had something*

---

[1]Blueprint for Life, 58.

different in mind? . . . I'm going to fill up blank paper this afternoon, writing stories—not just any stories, but my story, played out in a number of different ways.

My only rule is to approach it like a biographer, as if someone is documenting my life from death backward. . . . First I'll write it like I have no knowledge of what I can't do, writing like I believe I am capable of all things. . . . Then, if it doesn't stress me out, I'll write it the way it actually has been, taking into account my fears and perceived limitations. I'll carry out my present to its logical conclusion, just as it has been lived up until now. . . . I won't edit I will just write. . . . I'm going to write it out in time increments, like "One year from now, I will be . . ." I will finish the story out however it occurs to me, but I'll cover the details like where I'll be living, what I'll be doing, what I will look like, how I will feel, what my accomplishments will be, who my friends will be, what I will be doing to relax, and other things that might seem important to note. Then I will write the same story for five, ten, twenty, thirty, forty—even fifty years from now.[2]

Margaret's approach was a lot more appealing to me because it allowed me to break my vision down into increments of time. It doesn't have to be done all at once. I can handle the one-year plan and the five-year plan. Maybe once I get going I will be able to handle the ten- and twenty-year plans. Margaret's personal list, or at least what she disclosed of it, was very enlightening to Shannon and me, and it gave us the freedom to take our lists in any direction we chose. Margaret listed things as simple as wanting to own a golden retriever and remembering to

---

[2]Margaret Becker, *Coming Up for Air.* (Colorado Springs: NavPress, 2006), 53–54. Used with permission.

floss her teeth and exercise regularly as well as more serious goals such as where she wanted to be in her walk with the Lord and her desire to feed hungry children around the world—five hundred thousand to be exact.

Although Margaret's book is a recent release, her first list was written eleven years before the book came out. By the time the book was released she had gotten a golden retriever, remembered to floss her teeth almost every day, and been involved in helping to feed starving children. Several years ago she received an award from World Vision, claiming that Margaret had been able to help five hundred thousand people through her commitment to their cause. She had never shared the number on her list with anyone but God, and He helped her make that dream—that picture—into a reality. Writing her desires and dreams down helped Margaret outline her process of becoming. It gave her more freedom to be herself when everyone else was telling her to be someone else. She had a plan, and she was motivated to stick to it. Let's be honest here, if we don't reach all of our life goals and become who we really want to be, we don't want a written record of it. Writing things down helps us stay motivated to actually do them, and it provides us with clarity when it comes to how we can get there (hence the one-year, five-year, and ten-year versions of Margaret's overall life goals). Unfortunately, Shannon and I have met

> *Writing things down helps us stay motivated to actually do them, and it provides us with clarity when it comes to how we can get there.*

many Christians who wrongly believe people shouldn't dream with such an unlimited scope. Apparently best-selling author Angela Thomas has met some people like that too. In *When Wallflowers Dance* she wrote:

> *I have friends who think they're supposed to stay little in order to please God. Never have anything. Don't get too smart for your own good. Don't celebrate too loudly or too often. Don't make too much money. Remain hesitant and fearful out of some twisted version of reverence. Just calm it down for Jesus. Become enough, but not too much. You could get prideful. People might judge you wrongly. You'd struggle with selfish ambition.*
>
> *But Scripture teaches us to be free to become everything we can for the glory of God on this earth. No holding back. No limits when it comes to the kingdom of heaven on earth. You're free to make your body and mind and spirit into the best, most lavish offering to God you can give.*[3]

136

Don't you just love that? Be big. Be lavish. Dream large and always consult with and believe in the dream-giving God. He's the One who showed Abram miles and miles of land he would inherit. He's the One who gave Joseph the dream that his brothers would one day bow before him. And He is the One who helped Margaret feed five hundred thousand starving people. If you dare to dream and you write out a plan for how to get there—yet you give Him editing power—He will more than likely help you stay motivated until your journey is through.

FOR FURTHER THOUGHT:

1. What techniques have you used in the past to keep yourself motivated to accomplish something?

---

[3]Angela Thomas, *When Wallflowers Dance*. (Nashville: Thomas Nelson, 2005), 185–186.

2. Have you recently lost motivation to pursue something or accomplish something? If so, what did you lose the motivation to do and why did you lose it?
3. What is your opinion of Christians who are in the "spotlight" or who are widely visible? (For example, "I think they are arrogant," "I want God to use me like that," etc.)
4. Name an example of someone you know who is highly motivated. How does their motivation help them get to where they want to go?
5. Does your idea of planning ahead involve life goals or this week's to-do list? How does this affect your goal-setting habits?

DO IT NOW

Draw a picture (even if you aren't an artist) of yourself doing what it is you want to be doing. Make two to five copies of your drawing and stick them in places where you will see them often—car dashboard, bathroom mirror, etc. During a companywide contest to win a trip, Michael's co-workers drew pictures of themselves in Hawaii and taped the pictures to their laptops. They ended up winning the contest as a result of staying motivated!

> **"** *The most pathetic person in the world is someone* **"**
> *who has sight, but has no vision.*
> —*Helen Keller*

Michael and I (Shannon) debated on whether or not we should include a chapter on motivation *and* a chapter on vision in this book. The two seemed to be so similar—yet so different. Finally we realized they were different enough to merit their own chapters without being redundant.

Motivation gets you started, but vision gets you through. Your vision must be proactive where, many times, your motivation is reactive. Like when you are motivated to make a change due to a great sense of dislike for your current circumstances. Extensive weight gain caused me to get a personal trainer. Thoughts of wearing a bathing suit or hiking Mount Rainier with Michael and some friends this coming summer—and just the desire to have a healthy heart and body—cause me to keep her. Getting my trainer was motivation, keeping her is vision. If motivation is your starting line, then vision is your finish line.

Motivation relies mostly on the present, where vision is centered on the future. Motivation looks around and doesn't like what it sees. Vision looks ahead until it likes what it sees and moves backward from there. If I want to hike Mount Rainier without huffing and puffing, I need to increase my stamina now. If I want to feel comfortable in a bathing suit in the summer, I need to maintain a bathing-suit body all year. If I want a healthy and fit body at age fifty-five, I need to take care of it at age twenty-five. Do you see the difference between motivation and vision and why it is necessary to have the two? Motivation won't always produce long-term vision, but having a long-term vision will always help you stay motivated. That's why we talked a little bit about vision in the last chapter.

Pushing Through the Peanut Butter

My trainer, Jessica, has a phrase she uses with me when I am working out on the reformer machine. "Push through the peanut butter," she says to me as the motions get harder and my muscles grow tired. Sometimes life feels like we have fallen into a big vat of peanut butter—we feel stuck, and it seems like no matter how hard we try to move, we just aren't going anywhere. We all reach points in the process of reaching our goals that are just plain sticky and hard to press through. Where we were once motivated we now find ourselves losing heart. The process of moving forward requires so much effort that we truly begin to contemplate the concept of giving up. Pushing through just isn't appealing anymore.

Many people talk to me as though I don't understand how hard reaching their goals can be. They think that since my first book was published when I was only twenty that I just don't get it—like I've had it easy or something.

What most people don't realize is that there were almost two full years between the release of my first book and the release of my second one. Sure, it seems like a short period of time now that I am looking back, but it didn't seem that way when I was living through it. Back then it was a daily anxiety.

For a while I honestly believed I peaked at the age of twenty and would never write again. Those who were close to me during that time know I honestly felt as if God was done with me. That's a terrifying thought, especially since I was so young. Who wants to achieve their dream only to have it snatched away so quickly? My greatest fear was that I would wind up a sixty-five-year-old woman who was still talking about what she did when she was twenty. Not attractive—or entertaining. During that time I really had to seek God for a sense of vision. *Do I keep writing or do I quit? Is the project I am working on the one you want me to be working on, or am I missing something here?*

I had to keep pushing through the peanut butter. During that time I hoped to release ten books by the time I turned thirty. I spent time dreaming about what that would be like, and I envisioned the sense of accomplishment I would feel by doing so. On days I wanted to quit, I had something to hold on to, and I kept writing. Finally I got to such a place of peace with God that while I was speaking at an event I said, "I don't know if the book I am working on right now will be picked up or not. But I know I am in the center of God's will for my life, and that's all I need to know right now." Literally moments after I stepped off the stage and finished autographing a handful of books, my cell phone rang. It was my agent—

there was an official contract on the table and I was going forward. I honestly think God held back until He knew I would fully trust Him with my career.

Now, at the age of twenty-five, my tenth book will be released. So much for waiting until I was thirty. Many times God has bigger plans for us than we have for ourselves. The scope of His vision for our lives is much larger than our own. We just simply have to trust Him. Psalm 37:4 tells us, "Take delight in the Lord, and He will give you your heart's desires."

This is a verse I clung to during the time when my motivation was waning but my vision was still clear. What does it mean to delight in God, anyway? I think a big portion of it is embracing each day with gladness—pushing through the peanut butter of life without grumbling about it. It means being thankful for the wait and enjoying the journey as much as you would the final destination.

During a more recent time of darkness and uncertainty—when my motivation was gone entirely and my vision was quickly fading—I attended a conference led by prayer warrior Stormie Omartian. One of the topics she was speaking on was the subject contained in what was then her most recent book, *The Prayer That Changes Everything*. At this conference Stormie shared that the prayer that changes everything is the prayer of gratitude and praise. In the book she says:

> *Worship and praise is the purest form of prayer because it focuses our minds and souls entirely away from ourselves and on to Him. . . . It's exalting God for who He is. It's communicating our longing for Him. It's drawing close to*

Him for the sake of being close. . . . He inhabits the praises of His people.[1]

I left that conference still feeling as if the weight of the world were on my shoulders. But I decided to change my attitude. Looking ahead, I could still see a glimpse of the woman—and the writer—I wanted to become, so I continued to move toward my goals. I wanted to be a person of joy and gratitude. Humility was a quality I desperately wanted but sometimes lacked because my initial publishing contract came to me far more easily than it comes to most.

In the weeks and months that followed that conference, I regained my motivation. And as I did, the darkness that had clouded my vision began to lift—slowly but steadily. The more I prayed, the more quickly the darkness lifted. My prayers were no longer the prayers of a beggar asking God to let me have my way. Instead they were prayers of gratitude—during this time I literally walked through my apartment and thanked God for every stick of furniture I owned. I thanked Him for the food on my table, for my health, and for those I loved. Honestly, I thanked Him for every possible thing I could think of. True, I wasn't where I wanted to be, but I also wasn't where I could have been. There are worse things than having a still unfulfilled dream.

During that season of pushing through the peanut butter, some very raw nerves were exposed in me. For at least a month I think I cried every day—and my heart became softer than it ever has been as a result. I learned to

---

[1]Stormie Omartian, *The Prayer That Changes Everything* (Eugene, OR: Harvest House, 2004), 9.

appreciate the beauty of David's heart's cries in the psalms. And I learned what it meant to still have a vision even when I wasn't allowed to take a single step toward it.

By withholding any and every opportunity to move toward my goals during this period of time, God was able to work with me in a way He couldn't have if He had easily given me everything I wanted. In brokenness I was far more teachable than I would have been had I been left whole. In retrospect I can see I wasn't really whole before any of this happened—I was hollow, yet living as if I were whole. I emerged from this period of time in my life as a stronger writer and a more tender woman. At that time I didn't know that I was really being made into the image of what I wanted to be. All I could see was that I wanted something I couldn't have. That's often how God works.

Reading the Road Signs

Recently Shannon and I (Michael) drove to a conference where she had been invited to speak. Our destination was over six hours away from our home, but since we were making the drive together, it wasn't bad. A few hours into our journey, I found myself reading every sign we passed. "What road are we looking for again?" I began pelting Shannon with questions the closer we got since she was the one holding the directions and the map.

When it comes to getting from where we are to where we want to go in life, we need to realize that we are all going to pass a road sign that says Obstacles Ahead. None of us makes it to our promised land without passing it. Life is not that easy—God cares too much for us to let it be. Perhaps we have set our own mile markers along the road to help us chart our journeys. None of us fully out-grows our tendency to ask, "Are we there yet?" And as all of us know, the answer is never yes the first time we ask. Most of us are lucky if the answer is yes on the umpteenth try. Our mile markers may look something like this: completing my college degree—check; moving out on my own—check; finding the person I am going to spend the rest of my life with—check. The list could go on and on.

And with every marker we pass, our confidence grows as we realize we are closer and closer to reaching our goals. What about traffic jams and construction delays? They don't always appear on the roads we drive on every day. But they will appear on the road of life when we are trying to get from where we are to where we want to go, and they can really mess with a person's mile markers and sense of vision.

> None of us fully outgrows our tendency to ask, "Are we there yet?" And as all of us know, the answer is never yes the first time we ask.

During the writing of this manuscript, we lost Shannon's grandfather. He was a God-fearing man who loved to read all of Shannon's books even though reading became hard for him in his old age. His loss was felt greatly by all of us. It was five long months before Shannon's family even began to feel as if they could breathe again and that life would regain at least a small sense of normalcy. It seemed as though at every family gathering, Shannon's relationships with her mom and grandma (both of whom she is very close with) were affected by this loss. And just at the point when everyone began to feel as if life was becoming normal again, another family tragedy struck in the form of a car accident, and everyone was sent reeling.

"I can't handle this," Shannon said to me one day. "I feel like I just can't take any more. I can't think. I can't work. I can't even function. In the year when it seems like everything in my life is coming together like it should, I feel like I can't even enjoy it because I can't even move." As a happily married newlywed with five books contracted for the next year, Shannon thought she was well on her way to achieving her goals. And just at the point where she thought she was going to be able to switch into cruise control, she ran out of gas. There really was no warning.

The thing about vision that differs most from reality is that in our visions we don't ever predict any hardships or tragedies. Two weeks before our wedding, my mom was diagnosed with breast cancer. The Tuesday after I got married, she went in for surgery. For the first six or seven months of my married life, I watched my mom endure brutal chemotherapy treatments and the loss of her hair and strength. At the same time this was happening, Shannon's grandfather fell ill.

Our first married Christmas was anything but merry. It was downright hard. We cried almost all the way through the season. There was no road sign to warn us that this supposed "happiest time in our lives" was going to be tinged with great sadness as we walked in and out of hospitals and nursing homes. Those things weren't in our vision. But they happened. And we had to deal with them. The best thing you can do for yourself as you continue to press toward your vision is to prepare as much as possible for the heartaches and obstacles that will most certainly threaten to derail you.

Be Prepared

You are never fully ready for life's trials and tragedies. Almost no one expects a life-altering phone call on the day they receive one. We just don't pencil things like that on our calendars—we don't factor them into our plans. But we should. Now, I am not saying that we need to walk around living in fear of what could happen. But I am saying that we could all benefit from recognizing and acknowledging the fact that achieving our goals will not come as easily as we would like it to.

The only way to prepare for this is to alter our mindsets and attitudes to reflect a complete dependence upon Christ. If we do this, even in life's hardest and darkest moments when vision is all but gone, life will not be able to derail us and our hope will be secure. Hebrews 6:19 tells us that our hope is like an anchor for our souls and that it is both sure and steadfast. This hope "leads us through the curtain of heaven into God's inner sanctuary." What is this hope we are holding on to? It's the reality that in Christ we have access to God himself and that He is always at work on our behalf. Romans 8:28 promises that everything that is happening in our lives is being worked together for our good—not just for any good but for our personal good.

So what do we do to prepare for life's triumphs and trials that threaten to steal our vision? We hold on to hope. Shannon's parents are avid boaters, and we have gone sailing with them numerous times. Every time they drop the

147

anchor, their boat stays firmly rooted where it is. Even when the wind spins it in small circles, it stays where it is anchored. That is how we need to be—anchored in such a way that even when life knocks us around we stay headed toward our vision.

Perhaps your trial at the moment isn't something like cancer or death. Maybe it is directly related to your goal. Perhaps you failed an exam you needed to pass to move ahead in school or professional training. Perhaps you interviewed or auditioned for a position you really wanted and were turned down—and possibly even downright insulted. Maybe you sit under a boss, or have a parent, who constantly reminds you that you will never amount to anything, and you are starting to believe them. Those are all moments when your vision is on the line—and so is your future.

Shannon likes to tell the story of when she was a junior in high school and she took the Advanced Placement English exam for college credit. At this point in her life, teachers and others were already recognizing her writing abilities, and she was working toward her goals of publication. She wanted to graduate from college in three and a half years, and passing this test and gaining these credits would help her do that.

The day of the test she got so nervous that when she skipped one question so she could come back to it later, she forgot to leave that question on her test sheet blank. She continued to fill in the bubbles for the rest of her answers as if she had not skipped that question. She realized her mistake just as time was being called and she had to hand in her test. The entire second half of her test, or

close to it, would be marked wrong. She was devastated—
and she didn't pass. The next fall when everyone was talking about their test scores, Shannon remained silent. A
teacher asked her to stay after class and asked Shannon
how such a gifted writer could get such a low score. She
explained her bubbling error and understanding dawned
in the woman's eyes.

"But I'm going to fix it," Shannon said confidently.

"How are you going to do that?" The woman looked
at her curiously.

"I'm going to retake the eleventh-grade exam this year
when I take the twelfth-grade test. They let you retake any
of the exams in order to get a higher score." The woman
gave Shannon an approving nod, and that was the end of
their conversation.

The following spring Shannon retook the first test—
and passed. Then she took the second exam and passed
with the highest score possible. People who knew she
didn't pass the first year were astounded. Three years later
Shannon was invited back by Mrs. Cutler, the teacher who
had kept her after class, and she stood in that same class-
room where she had boldly proclaimed she would retake
the test, and encouraged a new generation of students with
her story—only by then, she was a published author.
Because she was determined enough to retake the test, and
she passed, she did in fact graduate from college in three
and a half years—five months *after* her first book came
out.

You cannot let your mistakes, and even your failures,
derail you. You have to keep going—you must remain
focused on your vision, and you have to keep your eyes on

the Lord. It is the only way you will ever get to where you want to go. If you know you have been called to do something great with your life, it doesn't matter how many times you fail—there is a guarantee that at least one time along the way you will succeed. You cannot give up anywhere short of reaching your goal. If you do, your vision will remain just a vision.

> If you know you have been called to do something great with your life, it doesn't matter how many times you fail—there is a guarantee that at least one time along the way you will succeed.

No one else can keep you on track. Sure, people can help you along the way, but they cannot do the hard part for you. Recently Shannon attended a book festival with her dad, and she came home really disturbed by one man she had seen at the event. He was an older gentleman who stood up from the crowd and began addressing a panel of authors during an open microphone session.

"For thirty-three years I have been waiting to ask this question," he began. "I have a story that I want to tell that will automatically make a bestselling book—and even a movie deal—and I can't find anyone to write it for me. How do I go about finding an author to write it without having anyone steal my story and make money off of me?"

Shannon said the panel of authors sat silent for a moment. Then finally one of them gave the guy some vague answer and blew him off just so he would sit down. Apparently Shannon and her dad had discussed it at length after it happened. But when she came home, she was still troubled by it.

"People like that just bother me," she said. "They want someone else to do all the work while they get all the credit. I mean, come on, he waited thirty-three years to find someone to write a book for him yet let him make all of the money. There's a book that will never be written."

We cannot let ourselves fall into the trap of dreaming a dream we are too lazy to pursue. Lazy people do not reach their goals. They lose sight of their visions before the visions even have a chance to become a reality. Everything is either too hard or too impossible to ever become a reality in the lives of these people. And as a result they live wasted lives. Lives full of "if onlys" and "I wish I hads." Do not let yourself live a life like that. You have too much potential. Your vision is God-breathed, and you have a hope strong enough to anchor your soul and help you hold fast to your vision even in the darkest of times. For you there is no excuse to settle for living life anywhere short of your vision.

Life is hard, but it is not impossible. Hold on to your vision and keep pursuing it as you pursue God. And one day, when your mile markers are all behind you and your obstacles have been overcome, God will look at you and give you the word you have been waiting to hear for a very long time: *now.*

FOR FURTHER THOUGHT:

1. What do you see as the main differences between motivation and vision? Why is it necessary to have both?

2. Think of a story—either fiction or nonfiction—where

someone's vision is what ultimately led them to accomplish a great feat. Then journal your thoughts about it.

3. Think of a time when your own vision for the future has grown blurry. How did you "push through the peanut butter"?

4. Think of tragedies that unexpectedly stormed into your life. Did they derail you from your goals, or did they grow you as a person? How so?

5. How can (or do) you overcome laziness in your life?

DO IT NOW

Write a short story casting yourself as the main character in a fictional role. Imagine you are a superhero—maybe not the type who can leap tall buildings in a single bound but the type who can overcome any obstacle. End your story with you reaching your final goal. Keep that story in mind next time life threatens to derail you. After all, God is better than any superhero, and He is always willing to fill you with His power when the time comes to push through.

> **"** *When people choose to withdraw far from a fire, the* **"**
> *fire continues to give warmth, but they grow cold.*
> *When people choose to withdraw far from light, the*
> *light continues to be bright in itself but they are in*
> *darkness. This is also the case when people*
> *withdraw from God.*
> —*Augustine*

We realize that nine chapters into this book you may have a clearer understanding of how to get from where you are to where *you* want to go in life, but some nagging questions may still be present, such as, "How do I know what I am *supposed* to do with my life?" And, "How do I know what *God* wants me to do with my life?"

Hopefully we have mentioned the Bible and the value of seeking counsel from a godly mentor or trusted friend enough times for you to realize those are two good places to start. Although we can tell you we are all here to glorify God with our lives (1 Corinthians 10:31), we cannot tell you how that will specifically play out in your life in terms of a career choice, a geographic location, or even a spouse. But we are confident that God will lead you to His answers if you seek Him. The Bible says enough about seeking God and asking for answers that it is clear that

God delights in answering the cries of those of us who care enough to know what His specific will for our lives is. James 1:5–8 says:

> *If you need wisdom—if you want to know what God wants you to do—ask him and he will gladly tell you. He will not resent your asking. But when you ask him, be sure you really expect him to answer, for a doubtful mind is as unsettled as a wave of the sea that is driven and tossed by the wind. People like that should not expect to receive anything from the Lord. They can't make up their minds. They waver back and forth in everything they do.*

Ask God the big questions and expect Him to answer— even if it takes more time than you would like for the answers to become clear.

So ask God the big questions and expect Him to answer—even if it takes more time than you would like for the answers to become clear. Since we cannot successfully or directly answer the big million-dollar question of what you are to do with your life specifically, we can address three key issues of life and how we can know God's will. The areas we want to address include your relationships, your church life, and your schedule. Even if you haven't answered life's biggest question yet, we are almost certain that these three areas exist in your life in one way or another. So these are good areas to begin uncovering what the will of God really is. Let's get started.

Relationships: Going Deeper

I (Shannon) am not a people person, although I can fake it when I need to. Big social gatherings like weddings, birthday parties, and church socials freak me out. Before I speak at a conference, I usually have some anxiety about spending so much time in front of a crowd. Honestly, people scare me. I have some scars from bad experiences with once-trusted individuals that make it hard for me to open up to new people. I'm a private person, and at times I can be a bit reclusive. (I am a writer, what do you expect?) It takes a long time for people to really get to know me. Most people who think they know me really don't, or at least not well. And in all reality I prefer it that way.

But the truth is, that is not God's design. Surface-level relationships stop short of what God intended them to be. Now, I am not suggesting that we become best friends with every person we encounter. But I do think we need to take most of our relationships to a deeper level if we are ever to make a difference with our lives. We can either spend our lives hiding from those around us, or we can invest our lives in those we want to impact and influence and those we want to be impacted and influenced by.

A certain passage of Scripture illustrates what I am trying to say. In Luke 24, two of Jesus' followers were walking along the road to Emmaus, talking about all of the events that had surrounded Jesus' death and (at that time) His "supposed" resurrection. Since Jesus had not appeared to all of the disciples, many of His followers were still unsure of what to believe about all that had transpired. Picking the story up here, it says:

> *Suddenly, Jesus himself came along and joined them and began walking with them. But they didn't know who he was, because God kept them from recognizing him. "You seem to be in a deep discussion about something," he said. "What are you so concerned about?" They stopped short, sadness written across their faces. Then one of them, Cleopas, replied, "You must be the only person in Jerusalem who hasn't heard about all the things that have happened here in the last few days." "What things?" Jesus asked.* (verses 15–19a)

At this point the two followers of Christ launched into a long discussion about current events. Giving Him a very surface-level rundown, they proceeded to tell Jesus all about His own death and resurrection. He responded to them by quoting passages of Scripture containing prophecies concerning the Messiah, but they remained sad and heavy-hearted. This surface-level conversation wasn't making a significant impact on them in any way. But look what happens next in verses 28–31:

> *By this time they were nearing Emmaus and the end of their journey. Jesus would have gone on, but they begged him to stay the night with them, since it was getting late. So he went home with them. As they sat down to eat, he took a small loaf of bread, asked God's blessing on it, broke it, then gave it to them. Suddenly, their eyes were opened, and they recognized him.*

When the conversation stayed at the surface level, it

helped the men pass the time as they were walking along the road, but it didn't make any real difference to either of them. There was no relationship that was being built. They didn't even recognize Jesus. It was only through inviting Him into their home and sharing a meal with Him that they saw Him for who He was, and their lives were changed. Encounters with Jesus Christ are the only thing that cause true life change to happen. And if our lives are meant to glorify God, then most certainly He intends for us to glorify Him in our relationships. That cannot be done if we are always hiding or sticking to surface-level conversation.

Think about how many times we meet people through work, school, or church. We see them every day or every week, and the conversation is always the same: the weather, sports, and current events. Maybe every now and then we throw in something we did over the weekend. But that's it. Many times we don't even know these people's last names. And if we are honest, we probably don't care.

After reading this passage in Luke, I knew I couldn't spend my life hiding like I preferred to anymore. Jesus demands more from us in our relationships with others. Especially in our relationships with those who don't know the Lord, we need to go deeper than surface level so that they can truly see Christ in our lives. Since I made this realization, I have tried to listen more when people around me are talking. Many times, when we make a more concerted effort to listen, we will hear things we wouldn't have otherwise heard. And we can take things deeper by speaking the truth we so readily know as Christians and speaking it into the lives of people who are hurting or confused.

The same is even true in relationships we have with other Christians. Recently Michael and I attended a church social gathering for people our age. Two guys began sharing that, although they are Christians, they have some real questions about the validity of certain parts of the Bible. We listened silently and nodded as they spoke, but we didn't really say anything beyond the surface level when they were through.

"I wish I knew them better," Michael told me, "because then I would invite them out to coffee and try to talk them through some of these questions they have." Why is that our mentality? For some reason we cannot seem to say, "Those are really valid questions. In fact, I had similar questions once too. Would you be interested in grabbing coffee with me sometime this week so we can try to talk through some of those questions you have?"

Remembering people's names is also important. At one event I spoke at a few years ago, a woman approached my book table and introduced herself. We chatted briefly and she went on her way. A few nights later she approached me again, and I greeted her by name (which is rare since I am not the best at remembering names, especially when I have hundreds of new ones introduced to me in one weekend). At the mention of her name she stopped and choked back tears.

"You remembered my name," she said. "I came up here this weekend feeling unnoticed and as if I didn't matter to God. I was coming over here to tell you that your book has really helped me see that I matter to God. But now I really know that He knows me by name and He knows just what I need." I was stunned. The simple act of remembering someone's name may be all it takes to affirm their value to them.

The people I have gone deep with in my life could probably be counted on one hand. But I can recall sitting through gut-wrenching agony with almost every one of them. One friend called me in the middle of the night and asked if I could come meet her. And in the darkness of the night she looked me in the eye and confessed that she struggled with a serious eating disorder. Another friend called in tears as she told me her grandfather had been having an affair. Immediately I rushed over to sit with her and hold her as she cried. The list could go on. But every time-tested and true relationship I have in my life has been marked by authenticity, by going deeper. Many times those same relationships were marked by the vulnerability of tears.

For me, crying happens in private. It very rarely happens in public or in front of other people. One of the only reasons I probably didn't cry with delight at my wedding was because there were one hundred people staring at me. When Michael and I were dating and I told my friend Krystal, whom I have known since I was five, that I cried in front of him, she turned to him and said, "She cried in front of you? I hope you know that is a big deal."

When we sit back and wonder what the will of God is in our relationships, the answer is almost always that we go deeper. That is where life change happens. It's where accountability takes place. It's where growth is encouraged and bonds are formed. And more than anything else, when we go deeper and risk vulnerability, that is where Christ appears in our relationships. And it is where He receives all of the glory.

Yes, there are times where we need to be careful and cautious about what we divulge to whom, but we all need to prayerfully examine our relationships and identify the areas where we can go deeper. In Genesis 2:18 God clearly states, "It is not good for the man to be alone." None of us can live a full life on our own—it goes against how we were designed. We were created to need God and need others—even if, at times, we don't like it.

> *None of us can live a full life on our own—it goes against how we were designed. We were created to need God and need others—even if, at times, we don't like it.*

Church Life: Pew Sitter or Servant?

Let's be honest here, there are not as many opportunities for twentysomethings (especially single twentysomethings) to get involved in the church as there are for other people. Many churches don't know what to do with those of us who aren't married—or who are married but don't have kids. Shannon and I (Michael) joined a small group at our church specifically aimed at young married couples without kids. *Perfect,* we thought. *Now we can meet people we can relate to.* Soon after joining we discovered that one couple was expecting a baby shortly, and the other couple was trying to get pregnant. *So much for that idea,* we thought as we kept looking for a way to find people who were like us.

But the key for us was that we kept looking. We loved our new church, even if we weren't exactly sure where we fit yet. The teaching was solidly based on God's Word, the worship drew us into the presence of God, and our church was making a lasting impact in our local community and the world at large. Our church was where we wanted to be. So when one small group didn't really work for us, we looked into other ways to get involved.

Finding a church you can call home can be difficult. That difficulty comes with the territory of being in your twenties. But one thing is certain: No matter how hard finding and fitting into a church may be, we are not—under any circumstances—allowed to give up. Sure, you may decide to try a new church. But you cannot give up on the concept of going to church altogether. Shannon attended a Christian university, and I went to Bible college, and we cannot tell you how many young people we knew who just gave up on going to church.

They had Christian friends and did Christian things; some even went to midweek small groups. But finding a church that had something to offer them was just too hard. So they quit. Small groups are good, but they are not a substitute for church, where you are under the teaching and shepherding of a pastor.

Hebrews 10:25 says, "Let us not neglect our meeting together, as some people do, but encourage and warn each other, especially now that the day of [Christ's] coming back again is drawing near."

Right there in God's Word it says, "Let us not

neglect meeting together." That means we are without excuse. It doesn't say, "Let us not neglect meeting together unless finding your place in church gets too hard—then it's okay to quit." A big part of finding your place means getting involved. If your church doesn't necessarily offer a special class or small group for your current stage in life, yet you like your church enough to stay anyway, then look for another way to get involved. Maybe the Sunday school, sound ministry, or worship team could use some help.

Shannon's friend Katie took a bold step in venturing out to find a brand-new church after graduating from college. Prior to that she had always attended the church her parents went to. Katie found a church where she liked the teaching and worship; it didn't really have anything for young people, but Katie stayed anyway. In time a group for twentysomethings was formed, and Katie became an integral part of putting that group together.

Sitting in a pew on Sunday morning and leaving unnoticed is not going to cut it. One of the reasons we go to church in the first place is for fellowship and accountability. You won't get that by hiding in a pew. Start small by committing to one extra thing at church. Volunteer to set up chairs. Attend a special event like a Christmas program and volunteer your time on the planning committee. Bake something for the church potluck. Attend a small group for your age group, and if there isn't one, see whom you can talk to about getting one started. But whatever you do, make church and a community of believers a regular part of your weekly schedule.

Priorities: Is It Possible to Have More Than One?

In their book *TwentySomeone,* Craig Dunham and Doug Serven make one of the most profound statements about priorities we have ever read. Here is what they wrote:

> *Our struggle is not as much a matter of time management as it is of priority management. That sounds simple enough, but our culture does us a disservice by pluralizing the word* priority, *confusing us as to what our priorities are and should be. Think about it: When we talk about our priorities, we're talking about something that doesn't make sense—remember the nature of priority is singular, not plural! We are only able to have* one priority. *The decision we have to make, then, is what that one priority is going to be.*[1]

So when you ask yourself the question, "What is God's will for my life?" you can always be certain that the answer involves making Him your priority. Jesus Christ is the best example of this. The Bible tells us many times that Jesus went to be alone with the Father. Before and after meetings with large groups of people, and in His darkest hour, we find Jesus all alone before God. For Him, time alone with God was a regular part of life. Gordon MacDonald once wrote:

> *Study the life of Christ, and you will discover that He was never on the verge of passionlessness. He obviously understood how one gets into that kind of situation. It is no accident that before and after heavy periods of activity*

[1]Craig Dunham and Doug Serven, *TwentySomeone* (Colorado Springs: Waterbrook, 2003), 138.

He went apart and stored up, or replenished, the inner energy or passion necessary to carry out His mission. And, again, it is no accident that He never seems to have engaged in activity that was beyond His reasonable limits.[2]

Life is busy, we know. You are currently rushing about trying to get from where you are to where you want to go in life. We know that too. But everything else is pointless if you don't get your priorities right—and eliminate the urgency of all those pressing things but one: time alone with God. That is the only way to come to learn the whole will of God for every single area of your life. It is the only way to have enough strength and energy to carry out all of the tasks that have been assigned to you.

We all have two choices and one life. We can either spend the life that has been given to us, or we can invest it. It's a lot like money in that regard, but it is different in primarily one way: When we die, our money stays down here on earth, and our life goes with us into eternity. If you had a sum of money that you knew would have to get you through the rest of your life because there was just no way to get more, would you carelessly spend that money, or would you invest it wisely and deliberately? We are guessing you would invest it, as that is the wise choice. So why would you do anything less with your life?

If you really want to know what the will of God is, you need to spend time alone with Him asking Him to show you. Jeremiah 29:11–14a says:

---

[2]Gordon MacDonald, *Restoring Your Spiritual Passion* (Nashville: Oliver Nelson, 1986), 34.

"For I know the plans I have for you," says the Lord. "They are plans for good and not for disaster, to give you a future and a hope. In those days when you pray, I will listen. If you look for me in earnest, you will find me when you seek me. I will be found by you," says the Lord.

Don't you just love the last part of that passage? " 'I will be found by you,' says the Lord." Anyone who picked up this book is honestly searching for more God in their lives. We all want clearer direction and a keener sense of understanding. We all want to get from where we are to where we want to go, and we want to be led there in triumph, not in defeat. We want to live full lives. We want to stop dreaming big dreams yet living small lives.

The best way to know God's will is to simply know God. And you do that best by spending time with Him in the ways we have outlined in this book. You have read the book, and we have given you the tools. Your time has come. Your moment to live the life you have longed to live is here. This is it. Your moment is *now*.

We will be praying for you on your journey.

FOR FURTHER THOUGHT:

1. In the past how have you understood the will of God? How have you made previous big decisions such as what to major in or whom to marry?

2. Do you currently have any deep and meaningful relationships? If so, what makes them so great and how do you contribute to their depth? Are there any relationships you can take deeper but are pulling back from? If so, why are you pulling back?

3. Have you had a lackadaisical approach to your career or job?

How do you think that has had an effect on your Christian witness?

4. What is your opinion of serving in the church? Do you feel obligated to serve? Do you think all church members should serve in some way? Why or why not?

5. How high of a priority is your quiet time with the Lord? How often do you meet alone with Him—once a day, once a week, once a month?

DO IT NOW

For two weeks (five days each), begin getting up five minutes earlier than the day before. By the end of the two-week period, you will have added almost one whole hour to your morning, which will allow you to spend even more time meeting with the Lord so that you can figure out what His will for your life truly is.

Due to limited space, we are including a short list of resources that may help you as you continue to make the most of *Life. Now.* For a more comprehensive list please visit *www.yourmomentisnow.com.*

Money Management:
The Crown Financial Ministries Money Map:
   www.crown.org/moneymap
Mvelopes Online Budgeting System:
   www.mvelopes.com
Debt Reduction and Wealth Building:
   www.daveramsey.com
Saving, Loans, and Interest Rates:
   www.bankrate.com

Goal Setting:
Blueprint for Life Small Group Curriculum:
   www.blueprintforlife.com

Wisdom for Life:
"A Father's Wisdom" six-CD series by Pastor Kenton Beshore. Order online at *www.marinerschurch.org.*

Fitness:

Healthy Cooking:
www.cookinglight.com
Fitness Magazine:
www.fitnessmagazine.com
Calorie Queens, Jackie Scott and Diane Scott Kellum (New York: Centerstreet, 2005).

Shannon Primicerio is the author of ten books for teen girls and has had articles published in *Brio* and *Marriage Partnership* magazines. She has been interviewed on radio and television programs across the nation and has been featured in such media outlets as PBS's *Religion and Ethics Newsweekly,* Crown Financial Ministries, *Money Matters* radio program, *The Harvest Show,* and *Time* magazine. She has a B.A. in journalism and a minor in biblical studies from Biola University and she has a passion to see her peers realize their dreams and live their lives for God's glory. When she isn't writing or speaking, Shannon enjoys going to the beach or watching a Yankees game on TV with Michael.

Michael Primicerio is a first-time author and a well-seasoned speaker who seeks to ignite a passion for Christ everywhere he goes. Prior to marrying Shannon, he attended Calvary Chapel Bible College and spent time studying at their extension campus in Israel. When he isn't writing and speaking, he enjoys traveling with Shannon and playing sports. A native of New York, he loves Southern California weather but remains an avid New York Yankees fan.

You can visit Shannon and Michael at their Web site *www.yourmomentisnow.com.*

Stop Dancing for the World's Applause and Step Into God's Studio.

We want to be liked—that's why we put so much energy into pleasing others. Life has become a dance that we perform for others, auditioning for a place in the hearts of everyone we meet. We put our energy into performances to please our parents, friends, teachers, boys—even people we don't know. It's simple: We all desire to be loved and accepted.

But in this busy, complicated world, we should be dancing as we were designed to—for the One who really cares. When the audiences are gone and we take off our masks, that's the part the Director likes best. Away from the alluring lights and demanding crowds, we can know ourselves and God in a powerful, meaningful way. When we realize that the One who matters already loves us, we will flourish in this life that is the *Divine Dance*.